T0204780

Selling to Anyone Over the Phone

Selling to Anyone Over the Phone

Renee P. Walkup
with Sandra McKee

Foreword by Karen Robinson
CEO of PrimePoint Media

AMACOM

American Management Association

New York • Atlanta • Brussels • Chicago • Mexico City • San Francisco
Shanghai • Tokyo • Toronto • Washington, D.C.

Special discounts on bulk quantities of AMACOM books are
available to corporations, professional associations, and other
organizations. For details, contact Special Sales Department,
AMACOM, a division of American Management Association,
1601 Broadway, New York, NY 10019.
Tel.: 212-903-8316. Fax: 212-903-8083.
Web site: www.amacombooks.org

This publication is designed to provide accurate and authoritative
information in regard to the subject matter covered. It is sold with the
understanding that the publisher is not engaged in rendering legal,
accounting, or other professional service. If legal advice or other expert
assistance is required, the services of a competent professional person
should be sought.

Library of Congress Cataloging-in-Publication Data

Walkup, Renee P., 1957–
        Selling to anyone over the phone / Renee P. Walkup, with Sandra McKee.
        p.   cm.
    Includes index.
    ISBN-10: 0-8144-7284-2 (pbk.)
    ISBN-13: 978-0-8144-7284-2
    1. Telephone selling.   I. McKee, Sandra L., 1952–   II. Title.

    HF5438.3.W34   2006
    658.8'72—dc22

                                                        2005011786

Printing number

10   9   8   7   6   5   4   3

Contents

Foreword

The number one predictor of successful salespeople is their ability to connect with their customers. In the years leading up to the present, the best sales executives have accomplished this by having multiple, face-to-face meetings. However, the demands on our clients' time, coupled with the increasing expense and frustration of travel, have minimized our ability to actually meet with clients.

Managers continue to look for innovative, but successful, techniques that can help our sales teams continue to connect with their clients remotely. This book has given a compelling argument that the old-fashioned telephone can in effect be "the most important selling tool" in today's hectic environment.

Selling to Anyone Over the Phone successfully conveys how the phone is critical to a sales person's success. More important, the book provides detailed steps on how to improve your telephone selling skills, regardless of whether you are selling a $50 yard service or a $500,000 new telecommunications system.

As an experienced sales pro, with twenty years as the CEO or head of sales for a number of companies that have sold everything from telecommunications products to early stage technology to alternative outdoor advertising, I was impressed to read the clear and powerful techniques that the author suggests. My team will now be implementing these techniques to reduce our travel time and expense without sacrificing our sales. You should too.

Karen Robinson
CEO, PrimePoint Media

Acknowledgments

To our SalesPEAK clients and seminar participants who trust us and make us sharpen our selling tools constantly—and who continue to profit from new ideas.

To my talented extended sales family: Dad, Mom, Aunt Carol, Grandpa Jack, and Grandma Flo, for providing me with the "selling genes" and for being role models ever since I started selling in downtown Kansas City at the age of seven. Thank you for helping me find the joy in a lifetime of selling and helping others.

Thank you to my dear husband, Ted, and our daughter, Rachel, for putting up with my long hours spent making the vision of this book a reality.

Special thanks to our diligent editor, Christina Parisi, at AMACOM for her enthusiastic support of this book. Last, I want to thank my dear friend/former customer/current mentor, Sandra McKee, for her organizational skills, excellent writing, and superb follow-through during this past year.

—Renee Walkup

I would like to thank Renee Walkup for bringing me into this exciting project. It was an honor to work with such a professional.

—Sandra McKee

Introduction

In today's selling environment, the telephone has become the most important selling tool next to a briefcase. For some reason, however, whether in outside or inside sales, very few people have ever had a class, instruction, or formalized training in how to use the telephone effectively to:

- ▲ Build immediate rapport
- ▲ Generate excitement about business
- ▲ Listen carefully for deeper meanings
- ▲ Control voice inflection and tone
- ▲ Close business consistently over the telephone

More commerce is being conducted now using the telephone. Even when face-to-face selling is involved, it all begins with the telephone call. For this reason, every sales professional in the world should have a phone-selling handbook to generate more sales. Just think about how the realities of doing business have changed.

With the ever-increasing expenses related to travel, more and more companies are bringing salespeople in off the "road" and putting them in front of a telephone. Salespeople who say they are more

1

effective in person are probably right. However, we aren't likely to get sufficient face time in selling situations if we aren't effective over the phone first.

How Effective Is Your Phone Selling?

So, what's bugging you about your phone selling? Have you been:

▲ Unable to uncover any new leads?

▲ Getting only limited information in your calls?

▲ Rejected too many times?

▲ Frustrated because no one calls back?

▲ Bored with making the same old calls to the same old customers?

If you answered yes to any of these questions, then the tools on the following pages are for you. The likely problem is that you have phone habits that aren't getting you anywhere. Perhaps the problem is that you are just starting out using the telephone for your customer contacts and want to close more sales.

Customers are busier than ever and are receiving more calls than ever— internally and externally. Thus, the well-trained professional salesperson must have exceptional skills to get a customer on the phone, gather information, build rapport, generate excitement, and advance the call to a commitment—the final step in the selling process. This process is often difficult to achieve in today's competitive selling environment.

A New Approach

In the past, many telephone salespeople were trained in a very aggressive—and not very consultative—approach to securing business. Most potential customers today are not only turned off by an in-your-face, dominant approach but are also enlisting increasingly elaborate means to avoid taking calls. *Selling to Anyone Over the Phone* teaches you how to effectively reach and become a decision-making partner with the customer. An important distinction you will learn in this book is the noncombative, constructive technique of the successful sales phone call.

Using personality matching and the consultative selling approach, you will become the kind of professional salesperson who can immediately identify a customer's personality type and match the customer's rhythm, tone and style, with the result of developing rapid rapport *over the phone*! The time for old methods that use lying, exaggeration, concealment, and manipulation is gone. This book will teach you how to sell with integrity, honesty, and warmth, thus building the kinds of relationships necessary for long-term customers and profitable sales.

The Challenge

Let's consider for a moment why effective phone selling is more than just dialing enough times that the percentages kick in. The following list shows what tools you have when you sell in person and eye to eye:

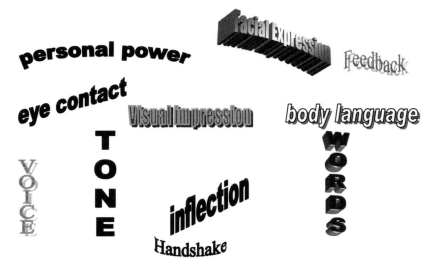

The visual nature of in-person selling allows us to use many means to create an impression: clothing, hair style, handshake, walk, and posture. Just our mere physical proximity to the customer makes the salesperson's job of establishing rapport easier.

Now, look at what is left in your tool kit for phone selling:

As you can see, establishing enough of a relationship with a customer to create a sale requires *very* skillful analysis of the customer's voice, tone, words, and inflection as well as precise strategic use of your own tools. You can "read" a customer's enthusiasm or reluctance in his or her facial expression and body language when you are in front of that person. On the telephone, you need to be able to interpret the subtle meaning of every variation of tempo, volume, and energy level as well as the words. Even the customer's pauses have importance.

In *Selling to Anyone Over the Phone*, you will learn the tips and finer points of phone selling as you become more skillful at using the phone to:

▲ Focus the customer's attention on your call

▲ Get the customer into a conversation and keep him or her there

▲ Generate customer interest in your products/services

▲ Get past gatekeepers and get them to *help* you reach your customer

▲ Ensure calls back from customers and prospects

▲ Set appointments and prevent customers from canceling them

Phone Selling—The Logical Choice

If you haven't been using the telephone for your prospecting, presenting, and closing, you are missing an opportunity to increase your effectiveness and your income dramatically. Think about the amount of time required to go see someone: getting dressed to create an impression, fighting through traffic, enduring whatever the weather offers on any given day, trying to fill the dead time of waiting. Add this to the expense of travel anywhere and you have a high cost of face-to-face sales.

But phone selling is different: no gassing up the car, no weather issues, no dead time waiting, and if the traffic is horrible, you'll still never be late for an appointment! Even if your main selling method up to this moment has been personal contact, think about how much you will increase your effectiveness and your revenue by "seeing" more people in a day. When you step up your skill at engaging customers and closing business over the phone, you improve your efficiency dramatically. All it takes is the time to read this book and practice the proven techniques it offers.

Polishing Your Phone Sales Tools

MUSICAL INSTRUMENTS have been around nearly as long as people have. The aborigines of Australia have the didgeridoo; Scotland brings to mind bagpipes; the American South has its banjo and fiddle. People use musical instruments to convey sounds of victory at sporting events, love at weddings, sadness at funerals, or enthusiasm in the form of lively dance. Musical backgrounds set the mood for movies, and in television advertisements, music helps to get the attention of specific target markets. As effective as musical instruments are in the hands of professionals, they can create merely noise when play is attempted by the untrained. Few people have ever been able to just pick up an instrument and make music come out. But most of us can, with instruction and the guidance of the notes on sheet music, play songs.

Think of the telephone as your instrument. Novices at phone selling make many mistakes and sometimes ruin their own attempts at the sales process. However, just like those who play music, true professionals gain success and expertise with instruction and become successful by practicing and following a well-thought-out strategy.

Taking Charge

Technologies such as Internet-connected cameras, text messaging, Web-posted slide presentations, and e-mail show a great deal of promise and might even be considered replacements for the telephone. However, each one has potential glitches and shortcomings. This standard technology, the telephone, is still the best because *it works*—landline or mobile phone, the technology works. You can find people, engage them in conversation, conduct business, and close sales over the phone.

Contacting customers and selling to them over the phone is a type of strategy game. It's a good game with a good payoff, because everyone has access to a telephone.

The strategy part of the game can be viewed as follows:

▲ Reaching people whom you do not know and might not normally connect with and getting them to speak with you on the phone. This allows you to get into the game, so that you have the potential to make a sale.

To do this, you need to retrain your mind to be quiet, to concentrate and make strategic decisions before you pick up the receiver. Each call might change your life.

If all you do to further your career and make yourself successful is integrate the skills from this one book into your sales techniques, you will have begun to take charge. *Selling to Anyone Over the Phone* will teach you to focus on strategies related to *personality* and *process*.

▲ **Personality.** Uncovering the personality type of each of your customers will help you to stop making assumptions about your buyers. Customers are not the same in their looks, buying decisions, needs, objectives, or problems. So, why would you use the same technique for each? In Chapter 3, you will discover four basic personality types that cover most of the customers you will encounter. You will learn how to build relationships skillfully, so that your customers are going to want to do business with you. When you reach this point, your satisfaction with your job will increase, you'll have more fun, and your bank account will grow.

▲ **Process.** In addition to building relationships with customers, you will learn a process that you can use in every call. It is an organizational structure within which you can use your creativity to keep in the game. As long as you are in the game, you have the opportunity to sell. In Chapter 2, you will learn about the acronym PLAYING, which will help guide you in the process to close more sales over the telephone.

Getting Yourself Revved Up!

Inside salespeople have more difficulty staying motivated, if for no other reason than because they stay tied in one spot to the telephone for long hours. It's hard work to sit and be motivated at the same time. Anyone who thinks it's a breeze hasn't done it.

Create a Motivation Zone

▲ *Move!* Use a hands-free headset so your neck doesn't become fatigued. Make it wireless and you will be able to walk around the room. Gesture with your hands while you walk and talk.

▲ *Improve your physical environment.* Spend the money on a good chair. Look at desk height and computer height: the ergonomics of your work area. This will reduce your fatigue.

▲ *Fill your head with positive self-talk.* Say to yourself, "I'm successful, I'm good at this." Play positive messages on CDs in your car.

▲ *Visualize success.* See yourself making successful closes: the customer is in to take your call, and the customer says yes. Do this when you go to bed, and each day before you start to call.

▲ *Read, study, and take classes in your craft.* Sharpen your intellect and thinking skills. Cultivate an awareness of other things going on and how they could affect your business or customers.

▲ *Listen to how people use their voices.* Add a button on your radio for National Public Radio and pay attention to how interviews are conducted; learn from people who are polished. You can even listen to ads on the radio to learn more about how people use their voices to communicate effectively—or not.

▲ **_Take meaningful breaks._** Walk outside and shift gears by studying different types of trees or just breathing outdoor air. Take a soda break, classical music break, exercise break, sports newsbreak, chocolate break, or a buddy break. Be sure to move away from your phone. (Just remember to come back!)

▲ **_Try something new._** Take a new tip from this book, for example, and integrate it into your regular day.

▲ **_Close more sales._** Get on the phone more, which will increase your total sales.

▲ **_Attend to your body._** Keep blood sugar at an even level by watching what you eat; get enough sleep—sleep deprivation clouds your brain; exercise.

▲ **_Reward yourself, not just when you close a deal, but also when you have stuck to your planned number of calls._** Pat yourself on the back; generate a reward system where you accumulate points to take yourself on a vacation.

The following ideas can help you climb out of the ho-hum pit— either ho-hum attitude or performance—during call day:

▲ Call a customer whom you like personally to energize yourself.

▲ Talk briefly to colleagues in your company about what they do to stay sharp.

▲ Rethink what you are doing. You may be burned out because you have developed some bad habits.

▲ Become aware of your tone of voice and your body language while on the phone. Are you having a bad day and sending a negative message? The month isn't over until the last figures are in.

The following drastic measures can be used to cure major or re-curring blahs:

▲ Consider whether it may be time to change jobs within the company or change products altogether.

▲ Don't blame others, the economy, the environment, the customer service department, or the computers, because pointing fingers will not motivate you. This attitude only supports you in your misery.

▲ Resolve personal problems. Any personal issues going on, even if completely unrelated to work, can sap your mental energy. Leave them at home.

▲ Investigate health issues. When your body isn't healthy, you don't feel up to par.

Finding Potential Customers and Classifying Leads

One area that doesn't differ whether you are selling in person or selling by telephone is uncovering leads. Leads are the lifeblood of the selling process and this is where your selling begins. Here are some sources of likely leads for your sales calls:

▲ Existing customers who are purchasing regularly.

▲ Inactive customers who have bought before but not lately.

▲ Prospects—people in your database who have been contacted by you or a predecessor in your organization but have not yet bought.

▲ Passive leads—generated by an inbound call to your company, from a Web-site registration, trade show, interest card from a magazine or ad, letter of inquiry, or a coupon.

▲ Referrals—generated by customers, employees, acquaintances, organization members, or prospects.

▲ Networking—being involved in associations, groups, face-to-face types of activities. These include alumni organizations, chambers of commerce, volunteer organizations, industry groups, training, or speaker events.

▲ Industry publications—magazines, articles, newspapers, local business publications, or online sources. For example, a company that announces that it is expanding its sales force could use new laptops or PDAs.

▲ Internal leads—from your boss, predecessor, colleague in a different territory; sometimes your customer service department is a great warehouse of leads.

▲ Lists purchased from third-party sources—these can be defined by target market parameters.

▲ Suppliers and business partners—people who sell in the same industry but are not competitors. Integration systems might refer leads to your software company, for example.

▲ Thomas Registry—classifies industries.

▲ Web searching—keywords, industry articles, and other searches.

Just as important as uncovering leads is the need to break down those leads according to their potential, to help you prepare a blueprint to guide your sales calls. Let's classify these leads into three categories for organizational purposes.

1. **Platinum Leads.** A specific customer's name and needs are known, or a direct referral whose name you can use. Existing customers are platinum, too.

2. **Gold Leads.** Information is available about these customers, but they are not currently active. They've called or sent in an information request card, but never purchased.

3. **Silver Leads.** You don't know anything firsthand about this one, but you may have read an article about a company that was expanding facilities or an article about a person whose company name was given. A generic contact.

After you locate potential customers, you need to be certain you are in your best skill form before you contact them. There are some basics you should keep in mind about phone communication.

Refining the Basics

Even if you have been selling for a long time, take note of how you can increase your phone power with these ideas.

Phone Power Posture

Sit straight; however, if you think better on your feet, use a wireless headset to allow you to stand and move around. For some people, this is a necessity because of their operating style. For most of us, however, movement helps to stimulate blood to flow—especially to the brain. Consider these examples: a choir sings standing up; comics perform stand-up; orchestra conductors stand.

When you stand, your diaphragm is open, as are your vocal chords, so you sound stronger and friendlier. This helps you come across as more confident and open to the person on the other end of the phone. When you are sitting down, with the accompanying restriction of air to the vocal chords and blood flow to the brain, you don't sound as confident over the phone.

Exercise: Play the outgoing message that you have on your phone message system. How does it sound? Were you feeling good that day when you recorded it? Were you standing? Were you sitting? Did you just talk or did you make sure that you came across with energy and receptivity?

After you have listened and analyzed your phone message, record a new one that reflects a clear voice, good posture, and energy level in order to encourage your customers to leave a message.

Write down your new message and practice reading it aloud, recording it several times until you sound professional and positive.

Voice and Tone

How do you feel before you get on the phone? Are you feeling up or feeling like the leftover of a bad day? Do not pick up the phone until you can sound upbeat and happy to be calling this customer. In addition to your good posture (head up—seated or standing) you need to smile to convey warmth and enthusiasm in those first few seconds, *because that is the amount of time it takes customers to decide if they will speak to you or not—only a few seconds.*

We've all heard how important smiling is when you are talking on the phone, but before you skip over this part, note the following:

▲ You sound friendlier when you smile while talking on the phone because vocal chords actually lift up.

▲ When you smile, the action triggers endorphins in your brain, which make you feel better.

▲ When you smile, you pull your cheek muscles up, making your diction clearer.

This may be a good place to address diction as well. Pronunciation is not just something for your old English teacher to harass you with. Clear, professional speech, without an extreme accent or noticeably poor grammar, allows you to communicate clearly to anyone in the English-speaking world. Casual speech with its local slang and variations on Standard English pronunciation can work—as long as you do not go outside your immediate community, industry, or age group.

If you call people from all over the country, though, you should be understandable to all your customers. The late President John Kennedy had a marked Boston accent, yet he was easily understood, as was former President Jimmy Carter, with his Georgia accent. The reason is that both moderated the extreme elements of their localized speaking styles and worked to ensure that they spoke clearly and with good energy at all times. Try this exercise below to help improve your clarity on the phone.

Exercise: To help you focus on the muscles it takes to speak clearly, place a pencil crosswise between your teeth and hold it there while you read the newspaper or one of your product descriptions aloud. Work at compensating for the obstruction of the pencil so that you can still be understood.

Is it difficult? Do your cheeks and lips tire quickly? That shows you how slack you have allowed those muscles to become, and that slackness is reflected in your phone diction.

> If you do this often enough, the muscles in your face, tongue, and lips will become stronger, so you will be able to enunciate clearly for longer periods of time.

If you have the luxury of some planning time between calls in your business, you may want to take a moment or two to refocus on your energy level, inflection, and pronunciation, especially if you are shifting gears by matching the personality type of your customer.

Maintaining Professionalism

1. ***Do not eat or drink while on the phone***.

2. ***Avoid vague wording*** such as "Yeah," "No problem," "We can do that," "No," "It's policy," or "No worries."

    Instead, use "Yes," "I'll be happy to take care of that," "It's a pleasure," "We'll take care of that," or "Here's what we will do."

3. ***Use can-do language*** by phrasing points in a positive way. Negative phrasing is insulting, even though you are trying to describe your customer's problem.

    Here's an example: The following phrase will sound negative to a customer: "I understand that your service people aren't converting service calls into sales leads."

    The following phrase will sound positive to a customer: "With a little training from us, your service people could be creating sales opportunities for your company."

4. ***Always be aware of your phone tone.*** You should sound competent and positive at all times. Remember to sit tall and straight or stand. Breathe deeply so that your voice resonates well across your vocal chords. This activity will not only make you sound better but also allows blood to flow to your brain, helping you to think faster on your feet.

    Avoid sarcasm in your tone because it can backfire. You could be the funniest person in your company because of your dry wit, but not everyone is going to "get it," especially when they can't see your face. Many customers don't know you, so your subtle humor may come across as offensive. Some comedians on the radio aren't as funny as they are on television. Body messages comprise a lot of the effectiveness of humor. Two people can tell the exact same joke; one is funny while the other is not.

In that same vein, avoid jokes; unless they are on you, they will offend someone. Humor can work, but not jokes. Blend your humor with your customer's personality. It's okay, in fact, preferred, to have fun in your calls. If your customers are laughing, they are more likely to buy from you! Make sure you smile when you use humor, so that the inflection in your voice comes across as playful and not snide.

When you establish respectful boundaries, you can begin to be a little more relaxed as the selling relationship goes forward. Just never get *too* comfortable. If your guard is down for too long, you are in jeopardy of saying something, or revealing a company secret or problem, that may come back to hurt your business relationship in the long run.

5. ***Demonstrate courtesy in your form of address.*** Always opt for a more formal approach in first calls, at least until the customer tells you otherwise: Mr. or Ms., Dr., Judge, Professor, etc. Some women might actually tell you they prefer "Mrs." but using "Miss" as a form of address has pretty much gone out the door in business.

Don't assume it is okay to use a customer's first name; however, there are cases where it may be acceptable. Voice mail may give you a clue. For example, "Hi, this is Jim," gives you a clue as to this customer's preference. Also, if the last name is difficult to pronounce, and you might offend the customer by mispronouncing her last name, you can opt for using the first name. In Japanese companies, sometimes employees will change their names in order to deal with American counterparts, such as "Tiger," "Bill," "Butch," and so forth, to make proper address easier. Always err on the side of formality until asked, or until the voice mail has given you a solid clue.

You can differentiate yourself by being more respectful in a world where graciousness is not the norm. We live in a casual society. However, some cultures are more formal than Americans typically are and might expect surnames for the duration of even a very solid business relationship.

6. ***Control background sound.*** Don't play music in the background so loudly that customers can hear it. If you use an on-hold system, it should not have offensive music or a general radio broadcast that might annoy customers. Classical music doesn't offend anyone, and you never have to worry about copyright infringements.

7. ***Choose the phone over e-mail.*** E-mail can be like playing the lottery. Although a great communication tool (the luxury of 24/7 availability), dependence on it can become your worst enemy. Since it's too often unreliable, e-mail as a substitute for the phone is risky. If you're depending too much on e-mail for setting appointments and for following through, you are wasting your time. E-mail, despite its convenience, is simply not a reliable form of communication in today's work environment. Also, e-mail is flat and nonemotional. You don't have the power of persuasion in e-mail like you have it over the phone.

In the worst of phone connections, landlines work. You may need to make a phone call to ensure receipt of an e-mail. Are you really going to depend on your quota being met through e-mail? Since eight times out of ten, a customer is shopping around, a misdirected e-mail can send your customers right to the competitor. The customer won't tell you he did not receive the e-mail or call to give you the opportunity to follow up. It is your responsibility to call and make the connection. (Maybe you should have called in the first place!)

> **Tip** Use fax machines; sometimes that works better. Since everyone is using e-mail, fax machines are less overloaded as an attention-getting channel. One of my clients used a fax recently to secure an appointment when telephone and e-mail strategies failed to work.

Selling with Integrity

Finally, if you are in this game of phone selling for the long run, you'll play with integrity. Even if you have many one-time customers or your sales are more short-term, you still need to consider the long-term implications of your actions. You will be able to sleep at night when your company is elevated in your industry and you behave with fairness, securing more business in the long run.

An important topic that seems most relevant these days is *selling integrity*. This topic comes up repeatedly in all my training sessions—whether the focus is on phone selling, presentations, or customer service. Everyone is searching for answers to the compelling question of: "How do I know when I (or my sales staff) have crossed the line?"

All of us have experienced a salesperson who lied to us in the past. It makes all salespeople look bad. We don't want the word *sales* to be viewed as a four-letter word.

Recently, one of my friends told me that they specifically bought their house so that their kids could go to the top elementary school in Atlanta. After moving, they found out that the realtor lied about the school district in which they now lived. So, rather than move again, they are sending their kids to private schools. That was clearly unethical on the part of the realtor.

Professional salespeople—at the top of their game—have everything to gain by operating with integrity. How many referrals do you expect this realtor will get from my friend? And the office that she represents is now tainted, too.

> Excellence is an art won by training and habituation. We do not act rightly because we have virtue or excellence, but rather we have those because we have acted rightly. We are what we repeatedly do. Excellence, then, is not an act but a habit.
>
> —ARISTOTLE

These days, your customers are more educated about your products and services than ever before. There is more competition than ever before. In addition, in most businesses, the sales cycle is longer than ever before. What does this mean to you as a professional conducting business over the phone? It means that you must stay on top of your integrity and communicate professionalism.

The following six ideas can help you to sell with integrity:

1. Always tell your customers the truth—that way, if you're not smart enough to remember a lie, you don't have to worry about it later! Over the phone, your customers can't see you, so they may be worried about your integrity at first anyway.

2. If you don't know the answer immediately, tell your customer that you will check into it and get back to him or her by a certain time. That way, you preserve your credibility instead of guessing.

3. Fact-check before quoting a price. If you give a ballpark figure on your product or service, it could possibly come back to haunt you later. You may have either overquoted, which negatively affects your credibility, or underquoted, which makes you look like a liar!

4. Make sure you understand what your customer's real need is. If you don't understand the customer's specific problem or goal, you may end up trying to make a square product fit into a round hole.

5. Remember that your long-term success is dependent on happy and loyal customers. Don't blow it.

6. Think before you speak. (Ever heard this before?)

The Payoff

Basic courtesy, plus attentive voice and phone management techniques, separate the real pro from the amateur. Less experienced and disciplined phone salespeople just wing it and hope they hit the sweet spot in the call, the point at which they realize the customer is going to buy. The very best don't rely on just talent or clever quips to get sales; they monitor themselves in their performance and technique constantly for areas of potential improvement. Customers have had enough of the hit-and-run brand of selling and are refusing to even take calls from anyone not believed to be potentially helpful to their situation. By observing the highest standards of phone voice and professional manner, selling with integrity, and gearing up to sell every time you place a sales call, you cross that line into the winner's circle.

CHAPTER 2

The PLAYING Process

IMAGINE YOU ARE at a French Quarter jazz club. There is a man playing a saxophone, or a trumpet, or maybe a guitar. He's alone, or there might be a single accompanist on a keyboard or drums. A stranger crosses the room from the bar, opens a beat-up instrument case, pulls out a guitar, and sits down next to the guy playing, looks at him, and gets a slow nod.

The guitar's sounds immediately blend with the other player's, and the two define harmony and melody in creative but perfectly attuned combinations. One leads, while the other pauses; then they take turns—leading, following, pausing, playing—always perfectly complementary, always without any notes on paper to guide them. They call this *jamming,* and it defines the perfect synergy that occurs when musicians and music come together in both creativity and respect.

If only all our phone sales calls went as well. We fight voice mail, Caller ID, and gatekeepers in order to reach busy customers, who feel harangued all day by other people calling them from both inside and outside their companies. It almost feels like we have to scream to get above the competition just to talk to a potential client! In music, they call that screaming *cacophony,* and it's pretty much the opposite of harmony.

People who know how to jam read the musical messages sent by one instrument and answer those messages by perfectly matching or blending responses. When was the last time you felt that a phone-selling situation was harmonious? And how would you like to have all your calls blend smoothly into closure?

Use a Process Strategy

The sign of a real sales pro is someone who can fall right into any selling situation and make it work. Here's the great news. You don't have to be born with a special gift to be this kind of a sales professional. What you need, however, is a workable strategy, based on careful observation; proven, workable skills; and a little understanding about achieving harmony in conversations over telephone lines with different types of people to generate more closed sales.

This book will guide you through gaining the knowledge and skills to be just that kind of pro. By the time you finish reading this book, you will be making your own kind of music with your customers. The following process acronym will help keep you on track:

P * L * A * Y * I * N * G

The success of this approach involves applying a process to every sales call with different types of customers. The result is more closed sales. In music, the notes, lines, and staffs are the same, but when the keys change, subtle differences occur in the way the melody plays out: sharps or flats may appear; notes may be in octaves above or below the staff lines. The process of PLAYING is similar—using basic skills and adapting them to the needs of various personality types found in customers. It involves *you*, understanding what motivates your different customers to buy and getting them to buy from you.

Plan for your call

Listen to the customer

Ask high-value questions

Yak less!

Involve your customer

Negotiate the close

Gain a Commitment

Applying this basic pattern *every* time you call a customer—whether you are cold calling, following up, making a courtesy customer service call, or thanking a customer for his or her business—will ensure that you make every phone contact count. Your customers are busy doing everything *but* anticipating your next call, and you are far too busy trying to keep up with your work to waste a single phone call. Getting the customer's attention is 90 percent of the sale in today's competitive selling environment.

By adopting this proven method, you'll find that you are more confident and relaxed on every call because:

▲ You always know what is coming next, because you have a proven strategy for every call using the PLAYING system.

▲ Your customers will respond to the process and not even know why.

▲ Your brain is disciplined to a system—ensuring that you don't forget a critical element of the selling process.

When the PLAYING process becomes natural and automatic, you will have more harmony in your sales calls because you'll make better customer connections, experience less stress, and achieve closed business faster than you have ever experienced before.

This systematic approach frees you to be creative as well as to concentrate more on your customers and turn more calls into sales. You will also find that customers respond in a more relaxed manner when you use a natural and logical approach.

This book is devoted to the PLAYING process, ensuring that you have the most effective tools for your phone calls. Now, let's take a look at this systematic approach one step at a time.

Plan for Your Call

Your goal is always to get the customer's business—either with this call or some subsequent call. In addition, you should have already done enough reconnaissance work on your client and his or her situation to know several things:

▲ When is the best time to reach this customer?

▲ Who is the gatekeeper?

▲ What challenges does this customer have?

▲ What happened when you dealt with this customer previously?

▲ What products or services is this customer using?

▲ How well did past sales attempts go with this customer?

▲ Does your customer have special interests outside work? (This information should be in your prospect database.)

▲ How is this person involved in the decision-making process?

▲ Who might influence this customer?

▲ What personality type is this customer?

▲ How will knowing a customer's personality type affect my call strategy?

Now, what about *you*? How prepared are you physically and mentally for this phone call? Before picking up the phone, do a quick personal checkup:

▲ Are you sitting up or standing in order to project the strongest phone manner?

▲ Do you have your customer information file up to date?

▲ Have you prepared your positive approach?

▲ Have you stopped and closed out any distractions before making the call?

▲ What is your energy level or mood at the moment?

Exercise: Using the previous questions, compare the diligence and detail you put into your current call planning with the guidelines given.

What is your conclusion? Are you already thorough in this element of your job, or are there some areas you can improve? If there is room for improvement, target specific areas. Refer to these as you go through the chapters in this book.

Planning involves an active process: goals, expectations, attitude, and organization. All of these can be improved with a professional awareness and discipline in making your calls.

Listen to the Customer

Now, with all this planning, and all the ideas you have collected, you will need to listen carefully to what the customer actually says and not filter what you hear. This means that the whole plan you have put together may need to be revamped on the fly when the customer intimates something different from what you expected. Remember the last time you were so focused on closing that you overlooked an opportunity or a key phrase that the customer shared with you? How well were you listening to the deeper level in the phone conversation? You need to focus on the hidden messages.

Customer interest selling *is* a conversation. It is easier to get someone to engage, when you let that person talk. Then, steering the prospect into your goal area topics will be much smoother—not to mention how much easier it is to get a customers to take your call when they know you will respond to them where they are mentally.

Keep in mind that all salespeople look alike on the phone, and with both internal and external salespeople calling your customer all day with their own needs and pitches, customers will remember you as the one who listened for a change. This subtle difference will make your call more memorable.

Suddenly, you won't be just another one of those people who calls with machine-gun blasts of feature dumps. In addition, you will clearly differentiate yourself from the customary interrogation method used by many strong-arm–type phone salespeople. You will be the one who "gets" what the customer is saying, and as a result, closes the sale!

Ask High-Value Questions

There are truly good and bad questions. In addition, there are appropriate times to ask these questions. Most good salespeople know how to qualify. However, only the true peak-performing salespeople know *in what order* to ask questions.

In general, *good* questions can do the following:

▲ Uncover information that helps you focus in on a need that can be solved by your product or service

▲ Help you build rapport with the customer

▲ Lead you to the decision makers or through the decision process

▲ Expose key areas before problems become objections

▲ Keep the conversation moving in the direction of a sale

▲ Advance the sale in every call

In contrast, *bad* questions can often:

▲ Cause the customer to feel pressured and thus end the call sooner than expected

▲ Close the information door, prohibiting further movement to discovering needs

▲ Damage trust and open communication, thereby destroying rapport

▲ Cause prospects to lie if too personal or invasive

▲ Offend people, killing any chance of a sale

▲ Leave the customer with a negative impression of you

A seasoned professional must have the ability to listen and qualify over the phone at a deep level. This topic is so critical to your success that this book devotes an entire chapter each to questioning and listening. What separates professionals from amateurs are good questions that:

▲ Elicit critical information from potential customers

▲ Build mutual respect and trust

▲ Lead you to closing the sale

When you ask questions that show you know something about the customer's specific situation or, at the very least, the customer's industry, you become a potentially valuable partner to that customer. Also, the customer develops respect for you and feels as if you know enough to not be wasting his or her time with stupid questions. Once again, this is one of your key differentiators as a professional.

By leading a customer to uncovering a problem or finding a solution to that problem, you are ensuring that the customer will take your call before others, and also that you will close more business faster. Open-ended questions starting with who, what, when, where, and how are fine. What about *why?* Why questions too often put people on the defensive. Why? Just ask someone close to you why they were late and see how this person responds!

You can often elicit *why* type information by starting with "Tell me . . ." instead. So add *tell* to the previous list. In fact, the more tell questions you ask, the more information you will get from your customers. This is our definition of high-value questioning. After all, isn't the objective to get the customer talking about his or her needs?

Yak Less

Most of the best sales professionals in the world got into trouble more than once for talking too much when they were in school. It appears now, though, that as professional salespeople, we've taken a perceived liability and turned it into an asset. The truth is that most salespeople love people. If we didn't, we wouldn't be in sales!

Now, as professionals with quotas to meet and commissions to earn, we are ready to funnel and control that energy in a positive way. We talk to build rapport, make our customers like us, and convey information. We just need to be careful not to have too many monologues! Remember, if you're talking, the customer is not; and when the customer is not talking, there is no guarantee he or she is listening to you. On the telephone, you won't be able to tell if the customer is listening to you, checking an e-mail, reading a lunch menu, or having a silent conversation with someone in the office. If the customer is talking, he or she is focusing on you.

Not talking can be an excellent tool in sales. A second of silence after a major point lets it soak into the brain of your customer; your pause midsentence can create anticipation. Being quiet after asking a question can give your customer time to think, so you can elicit more valuable information. Also, continuing to talk after the customer is sold can result in talking a customer right out of a sale, as shown in the following example:

> **Susan was on the phone with a large client and had gotten a commitment within the first three minutes. But in her enthusiasm, Susan kept listing benefits of the product. Eventually, the customer backed off, and the sale was lost. At some point, the customer heard something that struck a nerve or maybe just became frustrated with the perceived "yakking" of Susan's voice. Whatever the reason, the result was that Susan sabotaged her own efforts.**

For the most part, talking too much or too fast creates duress in the conversation. Hey, don't we have enough potential adversity in our calls already? Sometimes it is difficult to know what is too much or what is inappropriate. But long silences on the other end of the phone, either because you are doing all the talking or because the customer is not responding, will tell you that you may not be doing enough listening. Remember to ask yourself, "Am I talking for me or for the client?" Lastly, if the customer has to keep interrupting to get a word in edgewise, that's another clue.

Just because you know a mountain of information about your product, doesn't mean the customer wants all of it. In fact, the customer only needs to hear one thing: "How are you going to make me happy?" Period. End of discussion.

Involve Your Customer

Whenever your product or service lends itself to an interactive demonstration, help the customer take possession. The Internet and company networks have made it possible for you to be on the phone with a customer while explaining a slide presentation that the customer can access on your company's Web site. Alternatively, you can walk the customer through the order process with your software, take him or her to an online comparison, or a streaming video online. Perhaps you have a perfect opportunity to set up a face-to-face call for the demo at the customer's site.

This is one of those places in the conversation where the *customer interest* approach comes in. When you have uncovered an area of interest the customer has, immediately involve him or her in using or working with your product or service in some way. An example is asking your customer to walk through a demo site with you.

Make sure that every time you share a feature of your service to your customers, you follow it up with a specific benefit to *them*. Okay, every salesperson has been taught the idea of benefits at one time or another. But is the benefit you're giving them one from the marketing department's list or is it one you can connect directly to the customer's particular situation?

A true benefit is a "what's in it for them" proposition. The bad news is that most salespeople provide a laundry list of features and forget to add the relevance to the customer. Making a comment such as "We've been in business since 1909" is irrelevant to the customer. You would need to follow up that comment with: "What that means to you is that we have been around for almost one hundred years, so you can enjoy peace of mind that we know what we're doing; reducing your lead time and stress." After you mention the benefit, ask for confirmation to keep the customer involved. We refer to this as the *check-in* or the F-B-C formula: feature → benefit → check-in, discussed further in Chapter 10.

Negotiate to Clarify Close

If the close is imminent, you might negotiate the customer's easy questions, such as "Is Tuesday delivery possible?" "Does it come in red?" "What's the lead time?"

On the other hand, tough questions are usually the objections. Classic objections include the following:

▲ **Inertia.** "We're just fine with our current suppliers."

▲ **Budget.** "That's not in the budget this go-around."

▲ **Quality.** "I'm not sure that's the quality that will work for us."

▲ **Price.** "Your price is just too high."

Questions or voiced objections let you know that a negotiation is in progress.

Objections are easily defined: Anything that isn't a yes is an objection—whether voiced or unvoiced. However, if your customers have no questions, they're not involved in the sales process. How many times have you heard the following:

Salesperson: Do you have any questions?

Customer: No, I'm okay.

At least with questions, the negotiation is still open, and a clever salesperson can parlay that into a close. After "No, I'm okay," all you have left is "Well, thank you for your time." How much commission do you think you'll get from this call? Worse yet, you'll probably never get another connection with this person the next time you try.

It isn't always easy to determine if the voiced objection or question is a real concern or just a smokescreen, or maybe just a way to get you off the phone. Whatever the question or objection, even if it is one you've heard countless times, treat it as if it is real and handle it. In Chapter 9, you will learn four methods to handle many specific objections (as well as those "We're okay" responses). The better you become at negotiation, the shorter your closing times will be, translating into more closes per day.

Gain a Commitment

The commitment stage is the close to the call. As noted in the previous section, the phrase, "Thank you for your time," is not an acceptable close. There are many types of closes, including the following:

- ▲ Signature on a purchase order
- ▲ Agreement for an in-person appointment
- ▲ Time set for a formal presentation
- ▲ Acceptance of a pilot, trial, or use of a sample

If you do not effectively close, you have lost your gold. Create or affirm an opportunity to make a return call by setting a date or some sort of confirmation. Remember, your customer is not thinking about you, so some way of moving the commitment to the front of the customer's mind is imperative. For example, ask the customer to take out his or her calendar to record it while on the phone. In this way, both of you are clear about what is going to happen next.

The key to making a close that sticks is taking it a step further, beyond the mere agreement. Play out with the customer the mechanics of how the sale is going to happen. The customer may need to act by a certain date to meet budget guidelines, for example. If you set a date for follow-up, you can monitor the process.

For example, you might say, "Based on your implementation date, it's clear you need to make a decision by the seventeenth. So, I'll call you Tuesday. Is morning or afternoon better? Two-thirty? Okay, I'll call you on Tuesday at two-thirty." Then, you must be absolutely certain to follow-through on this appointment, as it is a crucial test in the mind of the customer of your own level of commitment.

If you tell a customer, "I'll call you later," you probably will not reach him or her. Setting and following through on times are signs of the true professional, and your customers will be more likely to honor their commitments to you when you make sure to do this.

The Payoff

Not only new sales reps but experienced ones as well can get caught up in the frenetic nature of the phone-selling situation. Salespeople often say, "I have to get it all out in a short period of time. Everybody's busy." So, instead of calmly and strategically approaching the call, the salesperson blurts out random benefits or loses focus during the call.

Think about how the line results of a lie detector test look. When the person in the chair is answering expected, easy questions in a truthful way, the line is smooth and flowing. But, when brain activity becomes frantic from confusion or second-guessing, the line shows up as erratic and zigzagged. Your customers perceive this seat-of-the-pants behavior in you and respond to it negatively. When you use a process, you are always in control and can remain calm and purposeful.

By using the PLAYING model, you are consciously controlling the call, and the customer is playing in harmony with you. You follow models all the time in your daily life. You don't put on your underwear after your pants, so why would you do your presentation before you qualify your prospect? The answer is that without a solid guide, you can become lost in indecision when things don't happen as hoped. (The word *hope* is appropriate here, because without a solid approach, a sale is just a hope.)

CHAPTER

Identifying Personality Types Over the Phone

IF YOU'VE EVER ATTENDED a rock concert where you were able to sit close to the stage, you might have seen a member of the band's crew off to the side tuning guitars. Energetic strokes by the lead guitarist can stretch strings slightly out of proper tension. In order to keep the quality of the sound perfect and allow it to blend with the other guitars and singers, the lead player regularly swaps guitars with the assistant who then hands the guitarist a freshly tuned instrument.

Setting up a guitar properly requires a tuning fork or an electronic tone device. When the sound coming from the guitar string vibrates at the proper level and matches the device, the guitar is said to be in tune. An out-of-tune instrument would sound "off" and would make the guitarist appear to be inept.

As a salesperson, however, being in tune with your customers is often the determining factor of a sale. You will be able to hit it off with nearly every customer when you use strategies that place you in harmony with your customers' personalities. Harmony equals sales. Learning to get on the same frequency as each of your customers will dramatically increase your close rate. Recognizing a customer's personality type may be more difficult over the telephone than in person, but there are definitely clues you can learn to identify.

Of course, it helps to understand what your own personality type is, as well. This knowledge lets you capitalize on your strengths with some customers, and manage your natural incompatibilities with others. For this reason, you will find a quick assessment in Appendix A that will help you to determine your type.

The personality types described in this chapter are generalities. However, once you practice some observations, you'll be able to recognize patterns in your customers, generally within one conversation and without being face-to-face.

To be the peak sales performer you can be, you will need to learn the following four categories into which your customers are likely to fall:

Precise

Energized

Assured

Kind

Remember, you *can* close each of these types with the right strategies. You may need to adjust specific things about your individual presentation style many times a day, as you talk with different types. This takes planning and attention, but the payoff means more dollars for you.

The **Precise** Customer

The keywords used to describe this type of customer are:

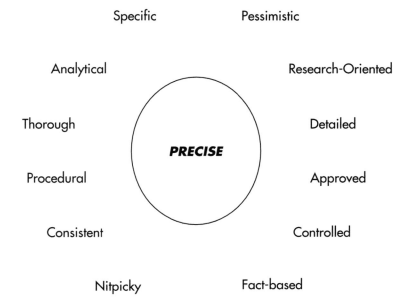

Specific   Pessimistic

Analytical   Research-Oriented

Thorough   Detailed

PRECISE

Procedural   Approved

Consistent   Controlled

Nitpicky   Fact-based

Characteristics

These customers need to be correct and certain about decisions they make and the implications of those decisions. Thus, they research and analyze carefully, never making a decision based on just their impression of you or a gut feeling. Because they have to "get it right," they are careful, never impulsive. Always seeking more information and wanting to be absolutely certain, they will even risk a deadline in search of convincing proof. After your call, even if you are able to gain a tentative agreement, the **Precise** customers will want to see a formal proposal. Under duress, they will avoid you, a decision, or a meeting, because if they are undecided, this feels like extra pressure from the salesperson.

These are the hardest customers to sell over the telephone. Even though you have satisfied all the possible impediments to a close, he or she will likely still want to see a written proposal. The logical nature of facts and computers makes them more comfortable with e-mail than with interpersonal situations. Task-oriented, **P** customers are generally very organized. In particular, they are likely to resent a phone interruption, so it is better to have an appointment for even a phone call for this customer.

Technical proficiency is a value to them, so fields such as engineering, computer hardware and software, accounting, and finance will have many people in the **Precise** category. Because of their expert knowledge, they are often consulted on decisions by higher ups, but will avoid major decisions on the company's behalf.

Over the phone, these customers may sound monotone, and you will hear this in their voice mail. You might become frustrated because they will not reveal emotions, even if they are enthusiastic about your product. To match a **Precise** style, you need to avoid too much enthusiasm in your communication patterns. Your phone style should be measured, deliberate, and controlled.

These customers think before they speak (unlike many of us in sales who think *by* speaking), so it may be common for them to be silent for a time after you ask a question; quiet even to the extent it might make you uncomfortable. The **P** customer requires extra time to process information. It's not an intelligence issue but a processing one.

These customers are proud of their own expertise and may be negative about the expertise of others. In character, however, they have a great deal of integrity, and although slow to make a decision, they can be counted on. These are the worker bees in their organizations and are often overworked and under-recognized.

Strategy

While **Precise** customers can be difficult to deal with on the telephone, they are by no means impossible. Be sure to give the **P** time to digest information; **P**s are not reactive thinkers. For example, while viewing a PowerPoint or information page on the company's Web site during a call, a classic error salespeople commit with **P**s is not letting this customer have time to read and study what is there. Huge mistake! If you have been successful in getting the **P** to your site (and you may get only one shot at this), he may sell himself if allowed to fully explore the information there. Be quiet and let this customer look at the material on the Web site. Silence on the other end of the phone is not necessarily a bad thing with a **P**.

Since you are giving the **P** so much information, be sure to organize it for easy access. As the expert, the **P** will not go to bat for you or your product in decision meetings, unless there is plenty of backup proof to substantiate the recommendation. (*Note*: This "once removed" situation, where someone will be your spokesperson with a decision maker is not uncommon in phone selling, especially with **P**s, since they are respected by others.) **P**s will not take the risk of losing expert status by expressing enthusiasm over a product they can't back up.

It is never good to surprise these customers with questions or calls, better to e-mail for an appointment and announce the nature of the call in advance. If you are a different type from them, s-l-o-w down and be prepared to match their deliberate and thoughtful pace. Temper also your own enthusiasm and any behavior that would rush a close or try to pin this customer down.

▲ Have the relevant facts and figures at your fingertips before calling a **Precise** customer.

▲ Answer all questions as completely as possible. If you don't have an immediate answer, call back if necessary, but as soon as possible.

▲ Avoid generalities and testimonials, unless you have one from someone the **Precise** customer knows and respects.

▲ Be prepared to send them proof, documentation, and articles from third-party sources (not press releases from your own company, but articles from industry magazines or tests by independent groups). A **Precise** won't necessarily take your word for it over the phone.

▲ Use a careful and strategic sales approach—it works great with this group, and follow-up often with regular contact.

▲ Give them time to think, though, and check for errors in anything you plan to say to them over they phone. If you don't, they are probably writing it down and will check your figures after you have hung up!

The **Energized** Customer

The keywords used to describe this type of customer are:

Exciting

Different   Innovative

Opinionated   Excited

Positive   **ENERGIZED**   Partnering

Dramatic   Referred

Benefit-Oriented   New

Happy   Recognized

The **Energized** customer will help you get your energy level back up if you're fading because they're infectious with optimism. Friendly, but hurried, they will talk fast and a lot. Using colorful words, they like to tell you about themselves and their projects, so they are not the best listeners. (Oops! Is this you as a salesperson? Need to watch that.) They are assertive and may even sell themselves on your product as they explore possibilities. Just remember to be quiet and let this type of customer talk!

Even at their fast pace, they are poor time managers and tend to be disorganized (you may need to assume they have lost something you sent). They also are not likely to take notes of your phone con-

versation and might forget important points. Because these customers respond well to people they like and can be impulsive as decision
makers, you can profit from this scenario if you cultivate their friendship. But, if they get mad at you, you will lose the business.

You will probably be calling more frequently with these people,
because they will want to build a relationship before they do business
with you. Because **Energized** customers are persuasive and opinionated by nature, they will typically provide you with referral business. You'll just need to ask!

Strategy

Energized customers will respond to your requests for favors,
"Will you just take some time to look at something for me? I'd appreciate your judgment and comments." Pay them compliments as
they like fueling their positive inclinations. These customers might
not have a referral's phone number handy, but they would probably
consent to a conference call and give a testimonial, if you ask. Remember, though, that under stress, they will blame outside forces
because they really see things as not their fault.

If your company has small promotional gifts you can send to the
Energized customer, these will be appreciated, as would any kind
of personal remembrance. An example would be: "I remember you
said your son liked P. Diddy. The radio station in our building was
giving away his single. I'll send one out to you."

▲ Send them brochures and customize materials and presentations as much as possible; use color. E-mails should be friendly
   and with bullet points.

▲ Stress the benefits to an **E** personally for using your service.

▲ Be sure your voice is upbeat and enthusiastic over the phone.
   Use more inflection and speak a bit faster—it may sound a bit
   exaggerated, but remember that the phone dilutes the effect
   of your vocal variety.

▲ Emphasize the relationship by telling them how important
   their business is to *you*. Convey the notion of team: Their success and yours are tied together.

▲ Remember to use thank-yous and use them often. Sometimes a phone call just to thank an **E** for business is a great relationship builder. A hand-written follow-up note is another good idea with these customers.

The **Assured** Customer

The keywords used to describe this customer are:

Powerful

Time-Saver   Results-Oriented

Revenue-Builder   Win-Win Focused

Cost-Effective   *ASSURED*   Goal-Minded

Market Leader   Opportunistic

Competitive   Expeditious

Efficient

Assertive and focused, this customer is all business. Although very opinionated, they are clear on what they like and don't like, and so are very decisive. They will innovate and experiment as it supports their vision. **Assureds** are committed to their goals and will go along with products/services that support those goals; however, they tend not to be loyal to individual sales reps or suppliers.

Strong leaders themselves, they respect those who have passed their tests and proven themselves worthy. They may not return calls, just to see if you have pluck enough to pursue them, or they might sound abrupt in a way that would scare away the fainthearted. They use the distance of the phone to their advantage. But to the victor go the spoils with this one, because these are often major decision makers and have the potential to be your best customers.

They may value time or efficiency over money, so be wary of the dollars-off approach as a sure winner. Because they are so time-conscious, if they suspect you will waste their time, they will cut you off. They aren't rude, per se; they're just serious about doing business, not engaging in chitchat. For this reason they avoid details, and so will want the short version or "executive summary." On the other hand, if you can handle with a succinct phone call what others want to do in person or in a rambling conversation, you will be able to get through when the competition cannot.

Strategy

Know their vision! The **Assureds** make their decisions based on where they want to go and what will help them get there. Be fast and well prepared and don't waste time with "How are you?" or any extraneous information. If you ask for ten minutes, note when ten minutes are up and offer to get off the phone. Expect that they are multitasking while on the line with you, so be prepared to reel them in occasionally or to do a quick feedback check to ensure they are still with you on the phone.

▲ Build credibility in your respect for their time, and they'll be more likely to take your calls. Expect to call many times to get through, because these are busy people who notoriously do not return calls.

▲ Keep your voice-mail messages brief and quicken your pace.

▲ Since time is short, speak their language to establish rapport quickly. Use power words such as *opportunity, important, your goals, timesaving,* and *competitive.*

▲ Avoid sounding fawning or obsequious by saying "please" or "I'd like to." Speed of execution is important also; you may get the deal because you act more quickly.

The **Kind** Customer

The keywords used to describe this type of customer are:

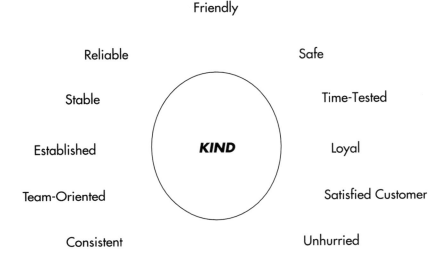

Friendly

Reliable   Safe

Stable   Time-Tested

Established   *KIND*   Loyal

Team-Oriented   Satisfied Customer

Consistent   Unhurried

Good Listener

Warm, compassionate, and people-oriented, **Kind** customers are good listeners and often a relief to talk to after some of the tougher types. They are unhurried and patient over the phone, never seeming to be rattled—even if they *are* under stress. However, be aware that these are sometimes your most challenging customers since they are so slow to make decisions.

Kind customers are loyal and will often stay with you, but are *very* difficult to get away from your competitor if that's been their association; they don't like change. **Kinds** will be warm, considerate, and agreeable, even if they are not going to buy from you. This can be deceptive. There can be cultural implications here, also, as some cultures feel it is disrespectful to be impolite or unkind to a person, whether there is any intent to actually do business or not.

Team decisions are more comfortable for this type, and **K**s will rarely go against the consensus. Under stress, you can probably get this person to say "yes" to give in, but "no" will be the real answer and you will get no follow-through. This customer needs time to make a decision that will stick in the long term. **Kinds** have often experienced being taken advantage of in past experiences, and this affects their ability to make quick decisions. It takes a long time to gain their trust.

Strategy

Because of the desire to be nice to all parties involved, this customer will need to feel that you will help him or her with others in the decision-making team. Recognize that **K**s rarely make decisions alone. You will need to find out who the other players are, but the **Kind** customers will likely happily tell you. Be sure to tell them, "Take your time," in your most patient voice and *mean it*.

- ▲ Ask these customers how their day is going and listen for the answer.
- ▲ Refer to something they told you about themselves in a prior call (there are excellent databases to help you keep track of these little personal details).
- ▲ Let them get to know you, personally, your company, etc. You will find them sincere in their interest; to them a product is the whole package—rep, company, *and* product. Knowledge on all these fronts will lower the perceived risk for **Kind** customers.

Most important:

- ▲ Don't push your **K** customers in your phone calls. They will give in under duress, but it will be a meaningless win on your part. They won't follow through, so the sale is lost.

Practice: Now that you are beginning to get a sense of these different personality styles, try classifying others you know or work with for practice. Each time you meet someone new or speak to someone for the first time on the phone, try to silently

(continues)

label that person's style as quickly as possible from your conversation. Then, after you have had a bit more time to get to know the person, check yourself to see if you were correct on your initial impression.

The more quickly you can assess a customer's style and adapt to it, the sooner you will be in a legitimate sales rapport conversation.

Tip Most customers' personalities are evident from their recorded phone message or their tone of voice when answering the phone. You can prepare for real conversations by listening to customers' voice-mail recordings. An opportune way to do this and identify the personality style is to call after hours and just listen. This will help prepare you for when you make the real call.

Personality Matches

As a salesperson, you have your own style and your own personality, whether on the phone or in person. By taking the Personality Type Assessment in Appendix A, you can get a clearer picture of your own type. In addition, you will be able to profit from understanding how to adapt your style to be the most effective with other customer personalities, by voice and style alone.

Remember, in love, opposites attract; but in our work life, we need harmony in order to do business effectively. Thus, we synchronize best with those who are most like us. When we meet our similar type, it's a beautiful world, especially when that similar type is our customer. We feel the harmony; we hit on the same notes, operate in the same rhythm. The phone line is almost a mental bridge between two minds.

Even when we meet our opposite, though, we can look for the elements we have in common. In the old days, phone salespeople were taught to get people to talk about their personal likes, so they could determine elements in common: sports, hobbies, kids, and so forth. Today's customers don't have time for such chitchat, but we can still establish that connection they require before they will do business with us. Instead of interests in common, we learn to pay attention to voice, style, energy, and inflection. Watch for the clues and choose your strategy accordingly. That's the quick way to the payoff.

Salesperson's Quick Reference Extra: The Salesperson ↔ Customer Match

Following is a guide for handling the different customer types, once you know your own.

1. The **Energized** Salesperson

E ↔ A If you are an **E** and the customer is an **A**, the elements you have in common are:

- ▲ High energy
- ▲ Aggressive
- ▲ Not concerned with details

E ↔ K If you are an **E** and the customer is a **K**, the elements in common are:

- ▲ Likes people
- ▲ Courteous
- ▲ Warm

E ↔ P If you are an **E** and the customer is a **P**, you have nothing in common naturally. For this *opposite* situation, you must change your style entirely. Of course, this takes a lot of energy to do, and choosing to go this extra mile when the stakes are high separates the big money salespeople from the lesser ones.

Remember: Most of us don't get to choose the customers we have to work with. Less successful salespeople spend most of their time with customers they like, whether those are the highest ticket customers or not.

An example of this is a salesperson whose clients are in the dental profession. She and most of her sales team are either **E** or **A**. Almost all their customers are **P**. The team had to work harder to have solid sales relationships with the dentists (their customers), but by adjusting presentation styles to fit the customer, they closed dramatically more sales.

A close on the large dollar account is the goal. It is very easy to feel good about a customer who spends money with you. So, the extra work it takes to adjust and perform more strategically is worth it.

2. The **Assured** Salesperson

A ↔ E As noted previously, you have energy in common.

A ↔ P You will find that you're both task- and goal-oriented.

The **A ↔ K** match was not made in heaven; you are opposites. What you need to watch out for is the **A**'s natural impatience with a **K**'s slower decision-making style. You may wonder repeatedly, "Why won't he make a decision? What's the problem?" The **K** you are calling may feel rushed if you are not careful to curb your tendency to push. Also, remember that the **K** is very loyal, and it will take you more time to get him or her away from a competitor.

With this match, if you give up too soon, you will *never* get the business. However, the importance of the account should govern how far beyond your frustration level you are willing to go before moving on.

3. The **Precise** Salesperson

If you are the **P** salesperson, **P ↔ A**, you have in common tasks and goals, and interest in the job done right.

For **P ↔ K**, neither you nor the customer makes rash decisions, both of you are more passive and precise, and with good listening skills between you. Although for different reasons, you are both somewhat cautious.

Look out, though, for the **P ↔ E** potential train wreck; you are *opposites*. Although contrary to your nature, if you don't communicate energy and passion for your product or service, you will not connect with the **E**. **E**s talk faster and are more emotional than you might be comfortable with. Control your inclination to be put off by that. Remember, also, that the **E** may close the sale quickly. Avoid the temptation to keep offering information and details; the **E** will lose interest, and you might lose the sale. Sometimes an **E** just "feels right" about a sale, and although this might be a foreign notion to you, relax and celebrate it as good news.

4. The **Kind** Salesperson

For the **K** salesperson, the **K ↔ E** match has relationships in common; you both like people. That's always a good start.

Ks and **P**s both want facts and don't move impulsively.

K ↔ A are opposite! The **A** will seem bossy and rushed to you. He or she will be abrasive and demanding in your eyes and will especially resent your desire to chat. Offer the **A** only the immediately relevant information and tie it directly to his or her goal.

Something that might help you deal with the **A** is to stand up when you are talking on the phone with this type of customer. That should motivate you to display more energy and enable you to set a faster pace. **A** customers need to hear confidence to conduct business.

The Payoff

Once you have mastered the art of recognizing your customers' personality types and matching them to your own, you'll find your telephone sales calls going much more smoothly. You'll be in tune with your customers and your sales strategies will flow naturally from this harmony.

Finally, the **P/E/A/K** salesperson—those of you who don't score as an exact fit for any of the four types—has an advantage. You will be able to move more easily among your different style customers. Just be careful that as you slip in and out of your different presentation modes, you don't get too cocky.

Being good at establishing a quick rapport with everybody does not necessarily mean you are the most strategic at closing the business. A more conscious awareness of the needs of each of the types will help you take all types to the next level and *sell more over the phone*.

Getting Gatekeepers to Work for You

IN AN INTERVIEW on public radio, a classical musician commented on a particularly complex piece by a contemporary composer: "It appears difficult, but once you learn it, it's not that hard to play." Very intimidating at first glance, the piece would scare off less tenacious musicians, who would choose something else to play for competitions or performances. Taking the time to learn the piece, the persistent player discovered the natural progressions in the notes, allowing him to offer something unique and complex when he played in public. What stopped most musicians was the initial, forbidding appearance of the notes on the page. Those same notes, whose arrangement came to make sense to the professional musician, offered a surer way into auditions and performances.

Decoding the complexities of gatekeeper selling situations and taking time to learn strategic methods of managing those situations can make you the master performer within your own competitive circumstances.

If you define a gatekeeper as the person or system between you and your sale, you will find many different types as you work through your daily sales calls. Each type requires a slightly different strategy, but each also is a threshold for you to move through to get to the real decision makers. Gatekeeper examples include **voice mail, automated PBX,** and **live people,** who might have varying degrees of involvement with your customer.

Voice Mail

Think of voice mail as the automation that most individuals and companies have to announce who they are and to accept messages.

Direct First-Person Voice Mail

Congratulations! In this case, you have reached the person's individual phone at his or her desk or a mobile device. There is a lot you can learn about your customer by listening to the voice-mail recording.

Here's a tip: If you know you need to make an important call on Tuesday to Jose Juarez, a very solid lead, call Jose's voice mail late at night, when you know he isn't there, and listen to his voice-mail message, so you can prepare for the call the next day. Using this method, you will be able to listen to the customer's voice recording more than once to learn his personality style from the voice-mail clues. For the actual sales call, it will be as if you already know him through his voice and can better plan for your call the next day.

As you listen, pay attention. Does he sound assertive and brusque or more passive? An assertive tone sounds forceful, confident, maybe hurried, direct, clear, and abrupt. A passive tone might sound more hesitant, careful, maybe detailed, has more filler words (uhm, oh, etc.), and typically pauses. This assertive versus passive determination is the first-level screen for you to identify the customer's real personality type—in advance of having a conversation.

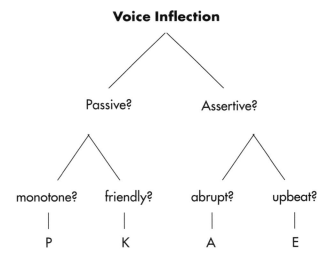

If the voice sounds assertive, the customer will be an **A** or **E**; if passive, the customer is either a **K** or a **P**.

The next clue you'll need to listen to is whether this person sounds abrupt, friendly, or upbeat.

As sound terse. ("This is Jose, leave me a message.") Notice how short the message is. **A**s do not like to waste time; they thrive on accomplishing tasks quickly. You might note that many **A**s also record their phone messages from their mobile phones (often on their way to the airport and going through a tunnel!)

Es sound more upbeat and animated, comparatively. ("This is Jose, since I missed your call, leave me a message and I'll call you back. Thanks a lot.")

If the customer sounds passive, this is a **P** or **K**.

Ps sound more monotone, remote, and possibly disinterested. ("You've reached Jose Juarez, leave a message or e-mail me at juarez @abcnet.com.")

Ks sound warm, calm, smiling, and fairly detailed ("Hello, you've reached the voice mail of Jose Juarez. Sorry I missed you. You may leave me a message and I'll call you back just as soon as I return to my desk later this afternoon. Have a nice day.")

The challenge for you as the sales professional is that in a real-time call (one you didn't do the night before as an inquiry), you have only two or three seconds to determine the type, and then make a decision as to how to manage the conversation. For this reason, prime yourself before each call to be ready to analyze and respond to a voice interaction. Be patient with yourself as you become accustomed to this process. You will learn to respond more quickly, just by practicing. It helps, though, if you are free of distractions each time and listening at a deep level so you can concentrate.

Leaving a Message You can prepare to leave a voice-mail message consistent with the customer's personality since you already know this person's style. Match the personality and delivery style: Your tone, inflection, speed, energy level, amount of detail, rhythm, and approach should be consistent with the customer's natural style. The purpose is to elicit a returned call.

Precise customers sound monotone, unemotional, and low energy. **P**s typically do not like to communicate over the telephone.

E-mail is their preferred contact method. So, it stands to reason that they sound as if it is almost painful to use the phone. This impression does not necessarily equate to their character or general happiness, but it does typify the way they communicate over the telephone.

If you are a high-energy person yourself, you will need to speak more slowly and deliberately for the **P**. Keep your message brief—between seven and twelve seconds—but resist the urge to speak too fast. If that's too much pressure for you to do on the fly, prepare in advance with some sort of outline for a message that fits that person, such as: "Hi, this is Renee Walkup from SalesPEAK, and I'm calling to briefly discuss your sales team. Call me at 678-587-9911." Remember to say your number S-L-O-W-L-Y. You are used to the number, but your recipient is not. No one will play the message several times to try to make out a garbled phone number. Even though that is generic as a message, you will need to change the energy level and tone to match the personality of the person on the other end.

For **Energized** customers, you'll want to match their style with an energetic, lively, compelling message. Use clear enunciation and an upbeat rhythm. These customers enjoy excitement and want to hear enthusiasm in your voice, tone, and inflection. Just remember to slow down when you leave your phone number! Your message may sound like this: "Hi Kathy, it's Renee Walkup with SalesPEAK and I wanted to get your opinion on an opportunity. Call me back at 678-587-9911. Thanks, Kathy, and I look forward to hearing back from you."

For **Assureds**, you'll match them with extreme confidence; be clear and quick. Use strong words, such as *need, have to*, and *call me*. Remember, uhms and pauses will make you sound less confident and professional. An **Assured** will pick up on this immediately. Also, avoid leaving a too-long message. The **A**s are the customers who are the least patient, have the shortest attention span, and that includes voice mail. Leave a message similar to this: "Gary, this is Renee Walkup with SalesPEAK. Call me at 678-587-9911."

Kind customers prefer pleasantries, a calm, warm, and friendly-sounding voice. Be unhurried. Take your time with these messages; feel free to include as much detail as necessary, and you'll find that you build rapport just in your voice mail. Avoid sounding too hurried, pushy, or "cheesy." These customers need to hear sincerity and caring in your tone. Your message may sound like this: "Robin, hi. This is Renee Walkup with SalesPEAK. Hope you are having a good day. Give me a call at 678-587-9911 so we can discuss an idea that may interest you. Thanks, Robin."

Variation on Voice Mail: Right Customer but Wrong Voice

Typically, someone of the opposite sex has recorded the outgoing voice-mail message. This is often done by an assistant, so you know an additional gatekeeper is involved, that there is a person between you and your customer, not just voice mail.

Strategy Since there is not enough information conveyed by this voice mail about the actual customer, see if you can get a receptionist or someone else on the phone. Identify yourself and say, "I noticed that Mel isn't answering his own phone; can you tell me, what is the best way to reach him?" Sometimes the person will give you an alternate number—including a cell phone!

Computer-Generated Mailbox Recording

This is either technically required by a phone system, or it is possible that the person is such a high **P** that she hates the phone communication. This customer will leave her name only to be substituted into the programmed message. In some cases, the reason for the computer-generated message is that the customer is an **A** person who doesn't want to waste time recording a message because she is too busy doing much more important things.

Strategy Listen to the energy in the voice. Use an even, generic voice and tone—not too energized or too slow—but use strong words to create a sense of urgency without sounding like it's an emergency.

Company Automated Menu (*No Information*)

Many companies are going this route to save money on receptionists or PBX operators. Perhaps you simply hear a robotic extension number or a computer-generated voice.

Strategy Listen for the options to reach a receptionist. Take the time to follow the menu to get to the person's extension.

> **Tip** If the specific extension for your customer is not on a list, opt for a person to help you secure the exact extension or number. Even if you get the wrong person, he or she might be inclined to give you the number—rather than transfer you to a receptionist, who has been trained to keep people (like us) out.

Live Person Answering the Phone

When you reach an employee, not the customer, professionally request to speak with the individual.

Receptionist

By definition, this person handles all inbound calls to that company. He or she answers for the company, then transfers calls. Company receptionists sometimes take messages; however, most often they move you into voice mail. Depending on the size of the organization or level of responsibility, this person may have a tremendous amount of information or may have nothing but an extension.

Strategy # 1 You need to find out what this person knows. How? Start a brief conversation with her, building rapport as you go. For example, provide partial disclosure to her.

Receptionist: ACE Construction, this is Linda, how may I help you?

Salesperson: Linda! This is _____. Is Rasida around this afternoon?

For a small company this is the best technique. You use a familiar voice to sound relaxed and expected. The receptionist often reads into your tone and inflection that you are a close personal friend of Rasida's.

Strategy # 2 If you are calling a larger company, your approach may sound more like this:

Salesperson: Linda, this is _____. Say, is Rasida Sandera in this afternoon?

Strategy #3 If you don't know the receptionist's name, say:

Salesperson: Hi, this is_____. I need to speak with Rasida Sandera. Is she in?

Use a familiar, friendly voice. Keep in mind that you are talking to someone who is treated like a PBX all day. Your personal and friendly voice is welcome as long as you don't overdo it. Remember to give *your* name first. Manipulative salespeople typically don't give their name. Receptionists are trained to ask questions in order to screen callers. By exchanging your name for theirs, you disarm the receptionist by not presenting an invasive front. We refer to this as the *full-disclosure method.*

Tip   Whoever is asking the questions is in control of the call. If the receptionist has to ask questions such as your name, your company, or what the call is in regard to, the receptionist becomes the controller of the call. We never want to have a barrier between us and the real decision makers, and we want to be in control of the call.

You should always sound like a professional on a professional mission. Don't offer your company name if it sounds too sales-y , but be sure to be forthcoming with your own name. Most of the time, receptionists don't ask for company names if you make it sound like Rasida is a personal friend. If you are asked, though, say the company name confidently, as if the customer would want to hear from your company. You may even disclose what business you are in, if the company name isn't obvious. This approach disarms a nosy, or well-trained, receptionist.

Strategy #4 If you have reached the receptionist during a follow-up call, say:

Salesperson: Linda! Hi. This is _____. Rasida Sandera wanted me to give her a call back today. Is she in?

Remember, only say this if it is true. A receptionist who puts through a call under false pretenses gets in trouble, and you have forever closed that gate. (Believe me, she'll remember your voice, company name, and maybe even have noted your number from the Caller ID.) You might choose to say:

Salesperson: This is _____. I'm returning Rasida's call; what's the best time to catch her in?

Sometimes they will put you through, or give you information on when to call back. A receptionist is an initial contact and has less of a stake in screening calls than other types of gatekeepers.

Exercise: Take some time to look over your contact list. How many of your calls fall into the category of *receptionist*?

Activity: Call three receptionists in your file and use the techniques described previously. Record the reactions you receive. (Check all that apply.)

▲   Attitude good
▲   Connected me to decision maker
▲   Responsive to questions
▲   Relationship established/improved

Administrative Assistant

Personal assistants have responsibility for a person or group of people. The assistant's job is to take care of the people to whom he or she reports. If a visiting vice president is on a low carbohydrate diet, the administrative assistant will ensure that low carb snacks are on the conference room table for a meeting. This is someone who knows what the bosses are thinking almost before they think of it. He or she can also be your most valuable ally.

Some customers are very dependent on their assistants for not only organizational matters but also decision making as well. In some cases, an admin can make decisions on behalf of the boss or help to push decisions through. In our competitive selling environments, where customers are busier than ever, never underestimate the power of an administrative assistant's influence.

Strategy Treat the assistant as a key decision maker who plays a central role in getting you to the person who signs the checks. However, assistants are well trained and have heard every trick in the book. So, throw out the "trick" book and use your professional strategy book. Be respectful and engage this person as your internal sales partner, the one who can make or break you. Ask the assistant the same questions you would ask the final decision maker. You elevate yourself in that person's eyes by asking meaningful questions and by directing those important questions to him or her. In addition, you are differentiating yourself from your competition by respecting the assistant's power; and you are doing this over the telephone.

It is helpful to find out how the assistant fits into the decision-making picture. How will your product or service affect this person or his or her boss's goals? You might find out that this assistant has had to field shipping complaint calls, which have become a personal irritant. He or she has to either handle or forward these calls and sees this as a nuisance. Now you know what motivates the assistant, and you can follow up on needs at several levels. Get the buy-in from the assistant, and the assistant will likely help you set up a phone meeting with the decision maker.

> **Exercise:** Take some time to look over your contact list. How many of your calls fall into the category of *administrative assistant*?
>
> **Activity:** Call three administrative assistants in your file and use the techniques described previously. Record the reactions you receive. (Check all that apply.)

(continues)

▲   Attitude good
▲   Connected me to decision maker
▲   Responsive to questions
▲   Relationship established/improved

Designated Adviser-Researcher

This key adviser to a decision maker is involved in the sales process but doesn't make the actual decision. Think of this individual as the researcher at a company. Often this scenario will begin with an inbound call to you. Years ago, the decision maker would call with inquiries when there was a need. Now, however, managers have much more responsibility in terms of numbers of people they manage, and they will delegate the initial search process to an adviser/intermediary. Often these information-gatherers are **P**s—detail oriented, thorough, and virtually unaffected by emotional decisions.

This type of selling scenario takes longer because you need to sell this screener/researcher. Decision makers will not talk with you unless this screener is convinced and has recommended your product or service. In this situation you must, in effect, persuade an internal agent to sell for you. This person must be educated to become your partner; he or she will present you, your product, or your service.

This is an important relationship because this person is your conduit to the sale. Never underestimate the intelligence and potential influence of these people. Today, they might be highly skilled, educated, and professional, which is why they are chosen as screeners. Highly respected, they are generally subject matter experts on whom the decision maker relies for information and recommendations.

Sometimes you might find that an intern has this level of expertise and respect in a company. For example, the intern e-mails you for information on your product. You call back and find that the receptionist doesn't know him, but thinks she knows someone who does. Eventually, you get the intern on the phone after laying the groundwork with all the others it took to reach him.

Whatever capacity this person is in officially, he or she is the one who can make or break you. Think of it this way. The screener is like the first door into the lobby. You don't get to the sixth floor unless the lobby door is unlocked.

Exercise: Take some time to look over your contact list. How many of your calls fall into the category of *adviser/researcher*?

Activity: Call three *adviser/researchers* in your file and use the techniques described previously. Record the reactions you receive. (Check all that apply.)

▲ Attitude good
▲ Connected me to decision maker
▲ Responsive to questions
▲ Relationship established/improved

Rollover or Call Forward—Colleague or Employee

Typically, in a smaller office there might be a vice president and a few managers. This could be a regional office of a larger organization. So, when a decision maker is out, he or she may just set the call forwarding to whoever is going to be in the office at that time. As the one who is just answering the phone when your customer is out, this person doesn't feel any great responsibility for relaying the urgency of a message. As an example, someone in accounting might receive a rolled-over call for human resources.

Strategy You'll want to first identify the personality style of the person who answered the phone. Typically, this individual may answer with just the company name, or their name. You are unaware if this is a marketing assistant, human resources manager, vice president, or operations director.

It's best to use the partial disclosure method by sharing your name and whom you are calling. Once again, use your warm, friendly tone and make it sound as though you are calling your very best friend in the world. The likelihood of getting through is increased.

Gatekeeper Partnerships

As you can see, with several of the previous possible call scenarios, you are going to be challenged to have a conversation with an intermediary, who can intentionally, or unintentionally, make your job a lot tougher. You need to engage these intermediaries in partnerships with you—either temporary or long term, depending on the situation. *And* you generally have only a few seconds to process that situation and strategize the best course.

Use as much care with these gatekeeper situations as you would with your customer, but be careful to avoid the old schmooze approach. Watch what you say, because there is a fine line between cheesy and "please-y." Cheesy will get you nowhere; please-y can earn you a partner who can make your job a lot easier!

How do you know if you sound please-y or cheesy? Listen to yourself. Record your pitch and see if you think it sounds sincere. You can also ask a manager or colleague to help you critique your approach. Lastly, you could register for a phone-selling seminar and test it out. See what the facilitator thinks of your approach for a more objective opinion.

Strategy Assuming you have a real person gatekeeper on the phone (versus voice mail), if you attempt the old-school approach of flattering the gatekeeper, you are in danger of sounding cheesy.

An example of cheesy would be saying (in your syrupy-sweet voice), "Oh, what a lovely voice you have, Mary." This will sound insincere, and if this is a busy receptionist, you are wasting her time. Also, reaching a gatekeeper who is a male and in a nontraditional role, such as receptionist or administrative assistant, may throw you for an instant. The professional approach works no matter who takes the call.

In contrast, the please-y strategy seeks to deepen the professional relationship with the gatekeeper.

Salesperson: Angela, I'm sure you're very busy. (Pause here just a second or two to see if Angela wants to tell you how busy she is.)

Gatekeeper: Why, as a matter of fact, I am. Tracking my boss's paperwork for travel expenses takes a lot of my time over and above my regular work!

Salesperson: I can understand. Our company has some really easy-to-use software that even your boss might feel comfortable with. Would that help you at all?

You see, just the fact that you acknowledged the duress many receptionists and assistants are under will differentiate you from other callers who treat them like a PBX. It only takes a few seconds to be supportive, and support is always welcome, unlike flattery. Later, in that call or other calls, you can likely expect a cooperative reception.

For example, let's say you are returning a call from a customer and reach a receptionist.

Salesperson: Keisha! Michael called me earlier. I'm trying to reach him, and I hope you can help me out. He said to call him at 10:00, but I haven't been able to reach him. Do you mind paging him, or should I call this afternoon?

In this scenario the gatekeeper might feel sorry for you, appreciate your honesty, and find the contact for you or give you a better number—cell or other location. As a sales professional, you can differentiate yourself from others who call and aren't professional.

A note here about formality is important. In other chapters, you have read that the more formal approach is better, meaning to call a person by Mr. or Ms. and use the surname. With receptionists and administrative assistants, however, we often only have their first name. They may answer the phone with, "Alexander Courtney's office, this is Pat." Or even say, "This is Kevin." Thus, calling Pat or Kevin by a first name would not likely be perceived as being too familiar or unprofessional.

> **Exercise:** Check your call frequency to gatekeepers.
>
> **Activity:** Take a few moments to write down some strategies to deepen your calling relationship with each of the gatekeepers in your contact list. Call more often? Involve more in decision questioning? Affirm in a more professional way?

E-Mail as a Gatekeeper

Your customer may have an assistant who serves as a screener for e-mails to save time for a high-level decision maker. To avoid e-mails that look like spam, make your subject lines intriguing, compelling, and professional, not too wordy. Obviously, you never leave a subject line blank. If you do, the spam filter will delete the e-mail or the customer will.

Faxes

You may decide to call or send an e-mail with the basic information, then fax the documents themselves. You might have better control over how your logo, formatting, and typeface look. Also, since faxes are not used with the frequency they once were for general contacts, they are often delivered right to the desk of the intended person.

The Payoff

Getting to customers is one of the biggest challenges of phone selling. Learning to manage gatekeepers as well as other obstacles such as alternate contact media will help you fast track to your contacts. Once you get to your customers, you have the opportunity to do what you do best—*sell to anyone over the phone.*

CHAPTER 5

Planning and Tracking

TIME AND MUSIC. How long is a song supposed to be? The radio standard is typically three-and-a-half minutes for a song. The longest number one song was "American Pie" by Don McLean, which clocked in at nearly nine minutes. Album-length CDs can have longer pieces, which are typically cut to fit the standard time if the song is released for radio play. It is fortunate that Bach and Mozart did not do their writing in the modern age of radio or the symphony might have taken on a very different nature. The reasoning for shorter songs is simple: Any time a song is playing, an advertisement is not on air. Too many long songs would cut into a radio station's ability to earn its advertising money.

For professional salespeople, especially for commission sales, time on the phone translates directly into money, while time not on the phone takes away from that income. Ineffective time on the phone can also spell loss in the long run. Planning, customer research, tracking customer information and accounts, and even skill enhancement (such as reading this book) are all non-phone expenditures of your time. When time is invested in perfecting your call-to-close ratios, that is time well spent and pays off in large dividends. Too often sales pros get lost in thinking they don't have time to plan or do follow-up tracking paperwork.

To learn what your time is worth, and to ascertain your value per hour, minute, and year, look deeper into this chapter. You'll probably find that every minute invested in developing your sales skills is time well spent; particularly if you work in commission sales.

Anything you do to improve your skills and effectiveness is a good expenditure of your time. Endless dialing of the phone that does not yield closed sales is not only a waste of time but also a waste of your own money. This chapter is about managing your accounts, and covers methods that will help you gather and utilize customer information so that your call planning leads you to more closed sales.

Information to Be Gathered

You need to keep track of a great deal of information about your customers. Since everyone's company does this differently, this section will be a guideline for what kind of information you need to keep and which methods work best to store that information for easy retrieval.

The following list shows the most essential information that's needed for easy retrieval:

Name

Title

Position

Phone extension

Mobile or alternative phone

Time zone

Fax

E-mail

Address

Their Company Web site

Some sort of status designation is needed: customer, prospect, referral, cold call, strategic partner, etc.

Sales history

Products/services used

Customer since (year) _____

Service agreements y/n

Renewals

Lease expiration

Follow-up date

Assistant's name/phone

Home phone

Personal interests—sports, organizations, or associations

Spouse name, children

Referred by

Personality type (**P, E, A, K**)

Best times to reach

Competitors—direct and indirect

Notes or comments section—captured conversations, dates, discussions, etc.

Link to a proposal or sales agreement if applicable.

Company Records → Getting Leads

Your company's intranet can tap you into forecasting programs, inventory pages, online slide presentations, or even customer service. These are good places to get leads. If your customer service personnel are trained to address service situations as sales opportunities, access to those records or personnel can lead to business for you. For example, recurrent technical problems could mean that a better or upgraded product would be appropriate. If a personal trainer has purchased home-use equipment and trains many clients all day on the equipment, he or she might be having problems with it, since it wasn't designed for such heavy use. For you, the salesperson, this knowledge gained from customer service might lead you to suggest commercial grade equipment, thus providing a valuable lead for you.

Take a look at who else in your company has opportunities to uncover leads? Who are your customers' employees contacting—such as other divisions in your company or from the service department? What might your boss or predecessor know about a customer? Perhaps one of your business partners or vendors knows about a customer's situation. Trade show exhibitors and attendees are a valuable source of information for many salespeople. Of course, you'll want to check the prospect's Web site and use the Internet for additional company or personnel information.

Do you know how decisions are made? Is the customer contact person a gatekeeper, purchasing agent, or does this person make purchasing recommendations?

As you can see, there is limitless information you can gather on a customer from behind the scenes. You will need to decide what is important, and more is often better. However, more information is only useful if you can catalog and retrieve it in a timely and purposeful way. The following approaches can help manage customer information:

Your Record Keeping

Paper methods can include index cards, call report forms, or paper files.

Advantages

▲ When you actually hold a pen or pencil and write down customer information such as interests, needs, and more, you retain the information for a longer term. Each time you process any type of data, your long-term memory kicks in, where it is easy to call back up.

▲ You might enjoy having hands-on control of keeping track of customers.

▲ If you are a visual person, you can use a color system of files or index cards for cataloging—past customers are pink, current large customers are green, and so forth.

▲ You can keep private any specific information that might not be appropriate for a company database. If a customer is a collector of baseball cards or refinishes furniture, you can keep this information. Specific quotes from customers or personal notes of yours about the personality or customer preferences become your private property, not to be seen by all company employees.

Disadvantages

▲ Individual pieces get lost.

▲ Paper/cards must be filed.

▲ Files, storage take up space.

▲ Information may not be easily transferable to someone else who might need it (sales manager, another rep, customer service).

▲ Management of hard-copy information can be time consuming—collate, file, alphabetize.

▲ Paper records are heavy and bulky, especially where there are many customers.

▲ Too much room exists for multiple errors (such as not being able to read handwriting, misplacing information, running out of space on a note card, etc.).

Electronic methods can include software, personal digital assistants, and computers.

Many companies have their own database system that programmers adapt from existing software or create specifically for their own company's use. Others use off-the-shelf products. An electronic management system can be as minimal or robust as you prefer. Since there is such a broad range of prices and applications, you should be aware of what you actually need. An interior designer who has a small business and must track fifty to one hundred clients might not want to pay $350 for a robust system when a $100 system might hold and track as much information as he or she needs.

Sometimes, though, less expensive software simply cannot handle the load. (Customer contact manager software such as ACT!, Gold-mine, Telemagic, and Salesforce.com are examples.) A recent search on Yahoo yielded thirty-five listings of Customer Relationship Management (CRM) software. Many of these programs can be put onto company networks, so your information technology manager might need to be involved in your consideration of which to choose. You can also find software that is compatible with personal digital assistants (PDAs). Whatever you choose, you need to ensure that your program is compatible with your hardware and software systems.

Advantages

▲ Established software systems for contact management have been around long enough for you to expect reliability.

▲ Portable devices are easy to use and to connect with desktop systems.

▲ Information is easily duplicated and backed up.

▲ You can keep records for a long time as a tracking and purchasing history.

▲ Many are affordable for individual use.

▲ Databases allow you to use many different identifiers to locate customers. For example, you might remember that a customer likes Californian wines and that you met the person at a telecom conference, but you can't remember the person's name. With a robust database, you'll be able to find that individual effortlessly.

▲ Data can be backed up regularly and easily to reduce the risk of lost information.

Disadvantages

▲ You may not have remote access to your database.

▲ Desired software packages might be cost-prohibitive.

▲ Information technology department might not allow software to be added to network.

▲ The software fields might be too restrictive. For example, you could find it useful to keep personality type recorded, yet the software won't allow added or edited fields.

▲ You might not have the staff or time to convert data—transcription, scanning, etc.

▲ You could lose your PDA or handheld computer.

▲ A virus in your desktop computer or on your company's network could cause you to lose everything.

Whatever contact manager software you choose, be sure it is flexible enough to allow you to create your own fields. One example might be "I.D." In this field, you could record how you know a customer. Maybe you met this person at a conference, professional association meeting, school alumni party, or even at the gym or in a class/seminar. This is also an ideal location to include a referral name so that when you call the customer, you can use the referral name. Sometimes, as part of planning, you will contact everyone you met through a specific association or at a certain seminar. You can customize a phone or mail campaign based on an approach relevant to those people in a particular organization.

You can also sort by fields to plan. In other words, you might decide that you want to plan your day by contacting customers in a particular time zone. Using your contact manager, you can call up people in those areas. It is important to have a consistent system for tracking what time you are to call, either their time or yours.

The way you are going to capture information isn't as important as the habit that you have created of gathering information and recording it. Being consistent with your record keeping is a valuable shortcut to your planning and follow-up.

Time/Cost Trade-Off

There are many ways to increase your efficiency as a sales professional. None, however, are magical, nor do they work unless you use them. For many of you, the recommendations in this chapter will be a significant departure from "I've always done it that way." The following chart will help clarify why it's so important to make changes that can improve your efficiency.

First, find your annual income in salary. You'll see to the right what an hour of your time is worth, a minute, and last, in a year, if you waste an hour a day, how much you have squandered in terms of time (based on 244 days per year). If you are on a commission plan, the numbers are even more dramatic, since there are wasted opportunity costs by not being as efficient as possible and maximizing your sales.

What is your time worth?

This chart shows a breakdown of the $ value of your calling time.

Annual Income	Hour Is Worth	Minute Is Worth	Over a Year What an Hour a Day Is Worth
$40,000	$20.49	.34	$5,000
$50,000	$25.61	.43	$6,250
$75,000	$38.42	.64	$9,375
$100,000	$51.23	.85	$12,500
$125,000	$65.10	1.09	$15,884
$150,000	$76.84	1.28	$18,750
$175,000	$89.65	1.49	$21,875
$200,000	$102.46	1.71	$25,000

So, the way you manage your time has a direct impact on your income. If you are on straight commission, or receive bonuses, that extra hour each day you might spend in the car running to customers' sites sucks up more than gas money. This is another good argument for making more use of the phone for your sales activity. Lost time translates directly into lost money for you.

Now, let's look at your day and see just where your time is spent.

Exercise: Where does the time go?

For this exercise, you will need to track everything you do for three days, rounding your activity to fifteen-minute increments. Let's say you start your day at 8:00, then spend one hour calling customers, then break for fifteen minutes, etc. Be honest with yourself because no one will see this but you, and its purpose is to help you make more money through greater efficiency.

At the end of the three days, sit in a quiet room and carefully analyze this report to see how you are using your time. Take a look at what you, personally, have control over.

Consider how you can make better use of your time in different ways. After tracking your time, you might determine that by simply starting your calls fifteen minutes earlier, which allows you to make eight more calls per day or forty more per week, you can increase your sales. This might lead you to close three more sales per week. If an average sale for you is $1,000, in a week that adds up to $3,000, which multiplied by fifty-two weeks equals an increase of $156,000 in sales per year!

8 additional calls/day → 40 more per week →
3 more closes per week @$1,000 →

$156,000/yr increase in sales!

If your commission is 10 percent, you've added $15,600 to your yearly income. Is that chump change? The discipline part of this, though, is that starting your telephoning just fifteen minutes earlier gets you those additional eight calls per day. If you already spend that extra fifteen minutes having coffee and reading the newspaper, you have only deprived yourself of fifteen minutes of sleep.

The key is to examine what you do with your time. Although each person is different, every sales professional can manage time more effectively. In your plan, you might take every Friday afternoon off. A colleague might see that as a waste of time. Yet, for you, that afternoon might be networking time (an important part of lead genera-tion), or it might be sanity preservation or exercise to stay healthier. If you spend fifteen minutes every afternoon talking to your child after school, that is not wasted time, even though it is a personal call—it is peace of mind. When you remember what your time costs, you are more aware of the cost/return ratio and what that means to you financially.

Taking care of your health, for example, in exercise, breaks, and getting out for lunch, is not wasted time. These activities result in better productivity. But if your friend doesn't like her job and she calls you to talk for an hour a day, that person is costing you money. In sales, there is typically a higher percentage of refusal than accep-tance, so you have to do some strict accounting to determine how to work the percentages. The way you spend your phone time is often the deciding factor. At some point, you need to seriously weigh how much money you need to make versus how much your time means to you.

Look at this time/expense trade-off example. Consider using a student or a sales assistant to manage your account information. A student might work for minimum wage as part of a co-op or for expe-rience. Start thinking about how you can maximize strengths and minimize the time commitment of things about which you are not as enthusiastic. It might be more cost effective for you to pay someone, even a professional temp, to do all the data entry, so that you can direct your time to getting on the phone and selling.

This discussion is not a judgment of your performance, or a rule imposed on you by a boss or manager. It is a choice—the kind of choice business professionals need to make every day. Just be sure you are investing your time and not just passing it.

Dispelling the 80/20 Rule of Sales

Every salesperson has heard of the 80/20 rule, that 80 percent of our business typically comes from 20 percent of our customers. It's amazing that we all seem to believe that this 80/20 rule exists no matter what our business is. Let this be the place where you finally hear that it may not be true. We've all heard "Brush your teeth twice a day." Like the 80/20 rule, that is only a guideline. You may need to brush your teeth more.

The rule presupposes a mathematical relationship. If your sales goal is predicated on 20 percent of your customers' business bringing in 80 percent of your sales, you are in danger of never making your goal. We cannot depend on history to determine our success because we live in a fluid world. Regardless of your industry, business constantly changes. Your best customer today may be acquired, merged, out of business, and your lowest revenue customer might expand. You could be blindsided by an unexpected turn of events, and you will have absolutely no control over being able to capitalize on the changes.

Your company may be rolling out a new product to a potential new market and you have no history of sales with that type of customer. The new customers might be the ones that will contribute the most to your growth. History is gone. Future success should be your focus. In sales, this is especially true, because the money from past sales is gone—either spent or absorbed. All that is meaningful for you in planning is, "What am I going to do *this* year?" Have you had a major customer that has gone out of business? What prime, top-of-the-line customer this year is one you couldn't even get on the phone last year? Begin analyzing your accounts to look for future business without presupposing the 80/20 classic rule.

Customer Prioritization

To determine how your are going to invest your time for maximizing sales, you'll need an *A, B,* and *C* customer identification matrix. Figure 5-1 shows a method of future account prioritizing that you might not have used in the past:

Before you begin your planning, you'll need to honestly consider where your best customer *potential* lies. By filling out the matrix in Figure 5-1 for each of your customers and prospects, you will find out how to invest your time to maximize income.

Consider these ideas when planning: What is your relationship with the buyer? On a scale of 1 to 5, your relationship might be a 4. If your competition has all of the customer's business, that would be

Figure 5-1. Salesperson's time management tool.

Accout Name	Cust.	Compet.	Relat.	Size	Maint.	Credit	Pot'l	Total	A, B, C
Example Account	5	3	4	4	4	4	5	29	A
Notes:									

Existing Customer of ours = 5

Competition has business = 1, we have business = 5

Size is relative to territory

Maintenance = time spent with handling complaints 1 = high maintenance

Potential = relative to territory

Total = Maximum of 35 points

A, B, C is relative to territory

Remember: You may weight any of the columns if you want, just make sure to be consistent!

a 1 on the chart; if you have all the business, that's a 5. Future growth potential may be a 5. You can total different categories and begin to look at all accounts. Maybe totals of 27 to 35 might be an *A* account, 19 to 26 would be a *B*, 18 and fewer is a *C*. This is a time-management and time-investment determiner, because you will never get your time back and planning is for *sales growth*.

Look at the future. Past *A* accounts might be maxed out, but *B*s might be in a position for greater growth. One other determiner from a time-management decision is "How high maintenance is that account?" If there are complexities, problems, or a high need for attention, it may actually be in our best interest to assign the account to a tech-person account manager or to customer service because the account might actually be costing you money in terms of your *time*. Remember, all these business-planning decisions are determined by time invested for the greatest result.

These are business decisions. If you don't have the freedom to choose these courses of action, make a case for a change and take it to your manager. A $12-per-hour employee can maintain an account, where your $80-an-hour attention for limited return might not be a good business decision. As a phone sales professional, you need to spend your time doing what you do best—selling on the phone, not maintaining already sold accounts that lack growth potential.

Let's look at an example of an inside computer salesperson, who secures a $1 million sale to a school district. The school district also needed a service contract worth another $300,000. The total sale for 2005 was $1.3 million. This is an *A* account for this territory.

Now, it's time to plan the new fiscal year. The salesperson considers this customer, an *A* account, then schedules the time in his calendar to work this account, say one call a week. A close examination, however, shows that it is, disappointingly, now only a $100,000 per year service account—not a priority at all. In fact, this customer won't be eligible as an *A* account for another two years after the existing contract is up. This account, in reality, has become a *B* or *C* customer. Calls from the salesperson to this customer for the current year should be strategically reduced and not disproportionately allocated by calling them once weekly.

What about you? Are you thinking past or future? Remember that phone selling is not just a matter of getting up and dialing from a list all day; you are not paid for the number of times you dial the phone. You are paid to generate revenue for your company, and subsequently for yourself. Companies base goals on projected revenues—not past sales. So, take a look at your *A, B,* and *C* accounts. You'll probably find that some of your *B*s are your best *A*s for the upcoming sales year. That some of your *A*s are now *C*s, because of buying patterns. Oh, and your *C*s can translate into *B*s and even *A*s. Take a look at your business and make these forecasting determinations. Just be honest when evaluating each customer.

Once you do that, you can strategically plan where you are going to invest your time, turning your calling time into dollars!

Now that your priorities have been determined, you have to parcel out your forty phone hours very efficiently. Because Garrison School (previous example) was an *A* account last year, too many salespeople would spend an *A* equivalent number of calls when the potential just isn't there. The result is wasted time that should be spent selling more to existing accounts and developing new accounts.

For example, in a forty-hour week:

▲ *A* accounts should take up approximately twenty-five hours of time (that includes planning, calling, leaving messages, having conversations with gatekeepers, and preparing proposals).

▲ *B* accounts require ten hours.

▲ *C* accounts are five hours. (You can often accomplish quite a bit with well-thought-out voice-mail messages, e-mail, and appointments in advance for phone conversations so that you aren't abandoning your *C* accounts.)

Remember, prioritizing is based on this year's potential, not last year's performance!

Creating Efficiencies in Daily Activities

With the million and one activities you do each day as you carry out your phone calls, there are probably as many ways to become more efficient. Some salespeople swear by wireless headsets. Some attest that a pen writes faster than a pencil. Putting *A* account numbers on speed dial is a good idea, but just ensuring that you have looked up all numbers for your call day in advance will make your day go more smoothly.

The following few hints can improving your efficiency. It will be up to you to determine what you do with the extra time.

▲ ***Monitor your personal calls.*** These calls not only interrupt your day for the duration of the call, they make even the most focused salesperson procrastinate about getting work accomplished. It may take up to a half hour to return to your pre-interruption rhythm. Set aside a slow time of your sales day to deal with your personal business. You will be amazed at how much more efficient you will become when you plan your days this way. Another benefit is that you can control the amount of time spent on these calls more effectively.

▲ ***Turn the audible signals off.*** If your e-mail box, PDA, or mobile phone is ringing, it is difficult to concentrate on the customer call. You'll be interrupted and wondering who's calling, whether it's important, and have other distractions. It will wait until your important calls are completed.

▲ ***While you are working, keep your file drawer open and your computer on.*** Have anything you might need during the course of your daily phone calls at your fingertips for efficiency. Organizational experts say to put the other items away where they are not distractions or clutter.

▲ ***Set time goals for yourself.*** "I will make twenty-five calls before ten o'clock." At the end of the time, get up and reward yourself. Be sure to plan your reward in advance, so you do not lose a lot of time figuring out what you would like to do! By stopping at the end of a goal time *and* returning to calling at the end of your break, you stay fresher and put more energy into your calls. Tired people dawdle. Better to plan time-outs and organize your day around calls, rather than calling arbitrarily until you are too exhausted to pay attention.

▲ **Clear your desk at the end of every day.** Things that become covered on your desk rarely receive proper follow-up. Hunting for misplaced reports, notes, or orders is time consuming. Reduce your paper by recording your call information regularly into your electronic tracking system.

▲ **Learn to use either hand for minor tasks.** There are many things that you could do with either hand if you made a point of it. Efficiency experts have noted significant time gains with people who avoid the extra movements required to reposition the body to use only the dominant hand. (Another reason to invest in a hands-free headset!)

The Payoff

Whatever method you use to make the most of your calling time, you are bound to improve efficiency. Far too many sales people never even ask themselves if their work could be managed better or more efficiently. If you are getting the same numbers, or worse, higher quotas on shrinking territories, you will have to improve somewhere. Addressing the management of your professional activities to make your time work better for you is money in your pocket and time for living a balanced life.

Setting Up for Success

NEARLY EVERY YEAR a different pop musician is accused of lip-syncing to recorded music instead of performing live on stage. One singer, whose career has spanned more than thirty years, often demanded a teleprompter so that she would never forget the words of a song she was singing in front of a huge auditorium of people. Although it may seem odd that professional performers "cheat" with these methods, they likely suffer from performance anxiety—the fear of making an embarrassing mistake in a public concert. For this reason, they use whatever support methods will help them be successful in giving the concert-goers what they want: a perfect show.

Most everyone who is in sales for a living has had to address the fear of what might happen if he or she "chokes" during a performance (sales call)—to put it another way, if the words either do not come quickly enough or they simply don't work. Even many long-time professionals have days where calling, especially cold calling, is stressful. When you have a plan that is likely to result in success, you look forward to the call experience, and your stress goes away.

Think of it this way. If you have good skills in basketball, don't you welcome the chance to demonstrate them in a game? When you raise your skill level and learn to manage all types of calls, then a call becomes another opportunity to be successful. This chapter is about developing a solid phone strategy.

Imagine that your goals are in place, you are confident, motivated, and prepared for success. That's how you begin each day when you are a professional telephone salesperson. Sound easier than reality? Read on to learn how you can start each of your sales days with success, instead of just coffee!

Prior Prep

You should do all your preparatory work the day or evening before your call day. If you wait to plan after you have begun your workday, you've already procrastinated! Planning saves time and maximizes your opportunities for a successful day of contacts and closes.

Call Planning

Start with a plan for contacting three times *more* customers than you think is humanly possible. For example, if your expectations are that you should make thirty contacts a day, plan on ninety calls. At least 75 percent of those calls are going to be voice-mail calls, which generally take no more than thirty seconds. Considering that, in one hour with good planning, you should easily get in thirty outbound call messages.

For some customer calls with which you need to confirm appointments, voice mail is an excellent way of handling them (see Appointment Security section of this chapter). With planning, you can take care of all these duties in a short time. That way you will be primed and ready to sell for every other call of the day.

Of course, if you consume five hours of your day actually talking to customers and closing business, so that you never reach the ninety calls, no one will be concerned. The key is to ensure that you are making the most productive use of your time as possible. Having enough numbers and strategy notes for those numbers in front of you for a call day prevents your wasting time and costing you and your company money.

Maximizing your outbound call strategy will yield more contacts with customers. Some you'll catch in their offices immediately, but others will be callbacks.

> **Tip** For those customers who regularly won't call back, put them in your plan on different days or different times of the day to increase the likelihood of reaching them.

Call Prioritizing To get your day going well, plan to start with an easy call—a friendly, low-stress, positive situation. For example, a good first call might be an upbeat thank-you to a regular customer. Another easy call to put on your list is to a customer who is expecting a returned call regarding an inquiry. This type of call should yield a positive response and get your day off to a good start.

After you decide what your first call of the day will be and the reasoning behind it, you need to prioritize the rest of the day's phone contacts.

▲ Priority #1—scheduled appointments, and also customers with the most potential to buy (not necessarily those who have bought the most in the past, but those who can give you the most *future* business)

▲ Priority # 2—key decision makers who tend to be in their offices at certain times—for example, executives often get to their offices early in the morning before the business chaos begins

For these early arrivers you may want to follow the same strategy. Call at 7:00 or 7:30 in the morning. Businesspeople are fresher, more alert, and less distracted in the mornings than they are later in the day when more has occurred. Someone who is difficult to reach or who puts you off in the afternoon may be more accessible in a morning call.

> **Tip** For these early morning calls, you may want to do a quick exercise workout first. Use the exercise momentum to propel you into high-energy calls. If you do your calling from home, even if you are all sweaty after an early morning workout, make a few calls, then go take your shower. Also, if you are prone to procrastination, this method gets you going!

Timing Considerations Also think about where you are calling to determine the best timing. In the Midwest and South, most people go to lunch between 11:30 and noon. In the Northeast (from Washington, D.C., northward) customers typically go to lunch around 1:00. Consider calling a decision maker, right before lunch. You would need to make this a short and efficient call. Also, you might want to intentionally catch a decision maker's assistant during the lunch hour. That way, you can spend some time picking her brain. Another alternative is to call *during* lunch when the assistant is out. Sometimes customers might even answer their own phone while eating a sandwich at their desk.

Also, remember your time zones. If there is a three- or four-hour time difference, you may typically be ending your day when most customers in another time zone are receptive. To avoid missing customers at their very best time of day, consider staggering your workday schedules—start early some days, extend later other days. Sometimes, if you are ahead of their time zone, calling your customers before everyone else gets going reduces your competition.

Other Time/Scheduling Considerations Ignore your colleagues who whine, "My customers don't work on Fridays." This is never true 100 percent of the time. To us, it's just a flimsy excuse not to work on Fridays. For example, most dentists don't work on Fridays, but mine does. Somebody, somewhere is working on Friday; you can count on it. For the decision makers who travel the most, Fridays are often the only day they are likely to be in the office. Think of calling the hard-to-reach customer at a time that is not routine for you. Think of reaching your customer at a time that is not obvious—especially to your competition!

The final step in time planning is to commit to beginning calls at a specified time. It's okay to allow time for morning exercise, coffee, getting kids out the door, if that is part of your personal day, but be very focused about the beginning of your *call* day.

Physical Space An important piece of prep work that most salespeople forget is the preparation of your physical space. Think about how it feels when you come home from a trip and the cleaning service has been there in your absence, as opposed to when you come home to disarray. The mess you leave in your workspace at the end of the day will not be magically put in order by the night pixies.

Time spent cleaning in the morning wastes productivity in your call day. A clean desk is *not,* in spite of what the adage says, a sign of a cluttered mind; it is, instead, the platform on which sales calling success begins. When your desk is clear of distractions, you are able to focus on your customer and the call—instead of the mess and all that you must accomplish. Most of us are easily distracted by piles of paper around us: memos, forecasts, reports, inboxes, magazines, and deadlines notices. In addition to paper pile-ups, computer tools are constantly notifying us of messages and work to be done.

Tip Turn off your e-mail message beeper and other audible tools that create distractions.

Guidelines for a Successful Call Day

Selling is a wonderful profession because it allows you to always earn a good living. It also allows you the freedom to be creative—in *every* call. You get to genuinely like people and have fun in your calls. What should be a part of every call morning is your positive mental success preparation.

Prepare for your day of success by making a decision the moment you wake up that you are going to have a profitable day. Positive self-talk helps. Look in the mirror and tell yourself: "I am a terrific sales professional. Customers *want* to speak with me and they need what I sell." This is the way you prepare your mental muscle for success.

Positive Expectation

Sit tall at your clutter-free desk and tell yourself, "Today I'm going to accomplish my goals." Be very specific about those goals. Your brain's expectations are powerful guides. If you tell yourself (and believe it!) that you will set your planned appointments, then your whole focus will be on carrying that process out.

One note for this mental preparation is to remind yourself that there are no such things as prospects; *they're all customers*. Now, say that aloud, right here, as you read this:

THERE ARE NO PROSPECTS; THEY ARE ALL CUSTOMERS.

If you think of them as prospects, then you allow for failure. Success with a *prospect* is somewhat iffy, subject to all sorts of conditions. Success with a *customer* is a done deal. You've already closed him in your mind, so the rest is just working up to that end! Calling prospects creates a "might" or "could" expectation. There is an adage that says, "Don't think, don't try, just *do*." Everyone is a customer, a "do," not a prospect or a "try." Positive self-talk will convince you that everyone will *become* your customer as a result of a conversation with you. This mindset will make your calls more successful.

Following your plan, remember to make that first call to an easy customer. If you have chosen a thank-you for your first call, don't forget to ask for more business or a referral while you have this customer on the line; it is still a sales call.

Using this technique at the beginning will set you up for a confident day of repetitive successes. Your attitude is good, so you are feeling confident, in control, and ready to close more sales! Then, if you have some disappointing calls later, they are a drop in the bucket. If you make more than three calls a day (and if you want to make any money, you are!), then likely some calls will be difficult or disappointing. That is just the numbers.

The point is where you place your *expectations*. Expecting positive outcomes frees your brain for creative thought and strategizing. Constantly trying to protect yourself from possible negative outcomes can paralyze you. The negative energy from all that defensive thinking alone is draining. In addition, your customers can feel fear or hesitation over the phone. When they hear a lack of confidence, customers have an even greater opportunity to shut you down, instead of becoming engaged in conversation.

Exercise: Fake it 'til you make it

Psychologists tell us that we can make ourselves feel strong and confident, merely by acting as if we are strong and confident. The next time you are having a bad day, instead of voicing that thought, put on your polished, confident voice— you know, the one where you feel like you're going to close in every call. Then see how the person on the other end responds.

You can even try this exercise with several friends and test it out. You just might become a believer of positive self-talk!

Energy-Level Maintenance

Take a five-minute stand-up-and-stretch break every hour or hour and a half. Movement is important. Do whatever you need to do to get your blood flowing and your energy up. Some people put on upbeat music and dance for a few minutes each hour.

Also, you should watch what you eat. Sugary foods and empty carbohydrates (such as chips, rice, crackers, pasta, and white breads) can cause an initial spike in energy, but then create a serious dip in an hour or so. During the workday, it might be better to eat small amounts of food at regular intervals. Complex carbohydrates (whole grains, vegetables) and proteins that are not heavy in fat (nuts, chicken, fish) are good. Avoid meats or tryptophans (turkey or milk products) because these foods have a tendency to make you sleepy. Citrus and sugary foods create phlegm, which makes you need to clear your throat or cough during calls, not making a great impression.

Use of Notes

Yes, you must take notes. Even the best memory won't hold details through two or three calls. You can miss quotes or the exact wording if you wait too long, and your notes end up in *your* words rather than your customer's. Be sure to copy down at least three or four *exact* quotes of what the customer says, especially where the "need statements" are concerned. Giving the customer back his or her own words as often as possible will help you to establish rapport and close more business because customers *love* to hear how smart they are.

Some people say they don't take notes because they stand while they talk on the phone. A tall table with a white board and marker or a blackboard will allow you to record important call details easily. Before you say that the fumes from dry erase markers or dust from chalk is offensive, smell-free markers and dust-free chalk are available. Flip charts work, especially for important customers whose information you may want to save and file. Or, if you use a headset or other hands-free device, carry around a pad and write while you listen and talk. Just remember to keep your head up.

Even if you are good with "super memory hearing" or if you feel distracted when you try to listen and write at the same time, you must still take notes. You can always write notes down immediately after you hang up. A word of caution: Don't delay writing down call information, because most people don't remember conversations very well, especially after time elapses.

Appointment Security

When calling to confirm an appointment, whether it's a phone or face-to-face appointment, here's a surefire way to keep from getting your appointment canceled. You don't want to be stood up, and at the same time, you don't want to create an opportunity for the customer to cancel either. Most customers are inclined to want to cancel because salespeople are not a priority in their work lives. Interruptions or disasters can occur, and priorities change between the time you secured the appointment and the real appointment time.

> **Tip** Remember, always confirm call appointments by using *voice mail*. If you leave an enthusiastic reminder on voice mail, the customer gets the nudge, but won't have an easy opportunity to tell you that his deadline crept up on him and he now must cancel your appointment. If you know when the customer goes to lunch, you can call at 1:30 to confirm on voice mail the appointment later in the afternoon. "Hello, _____, I'm looking forward to speaking with you at 3:30 today about an efficient way of solving your shipping problems." You can also call the cus-

tomer the night before the appointment, when she is unlikely to be in her office. Leave the same message.

But, be wary. If you have to confirm the appointment when Sam might be in his office, call the main switchboard instead of Sam's direct number. When you get the receptionist, ask to be forwarded to Sam's voice mail, not his extension. Then leave your message.

Another way to prevent cancellations from the reminder call is to *never leave your phone number when you call the customer's voice mail.* You don't want Sam calling back and canceling, so you are better off not making it easy for him. If the customer doesn't have your number handy (most don't), he or she won't call you to cancel.

These techniques will reduce your cancellations dramatically. If you are getting many cancellations, then you are not confirming, or you are using e-mail as a confirmation tool, or you are making it too easy for the client to cancel.

Tip Here is another appointment security tip. If you have been using e-mail to confirm call appointments, you might want to rethink that practice. That *reply* button makes it much too convenient for your customers to ask to be released from the appointment. Remember, their enthusiasm level is not the same now as it was at the end of your scheduling call. And, without that initial enthusiasm, they tend to revert to thinking they are too busy to talk to you. In addition, although e-mail may be your preferred communication medium, your customer may avoid it. Thus, a confirmation may go unnoticed. Lastly, with filled mailboxes and downed servers, e-mail is just plain unreliable.

Call Openers

Your call day is under way. Before each call you make, remember to take fifteen seconds to decide your goal, the personality approach, and opening statement.

Thank You

A lot of people are calling your customers to sell products, but very few people are thanking their customers for their business. For that matter, thank-yous seem to be falling out of our interactions altogether these days. For this reason, if for no other, you should offer appreciation to differentiate yourself. Your customer may just show his or her gratitude for the affirmation with a purchase order or a referral.

For an existing customer, the best opener might very well be a thank-you.

Salesperson: Ms. Johnson, this is _____ from _____. I want to thank you for your recent order.

Salesperson: Mr. Levine, I understand you have been purchasing from our company for five years, and I want to thank you.

This will disarm most customers because they aren't used to getting a call thanking them for business. It may be a judgment call on your part whether to "thank and run" to cement a good impression in the customer's mind. However, if the customer is responsive and jumps in to discuss business, then move forward. If the customer mentions being pleased with your product or service, then move forward. Sometimes, however, you might want to just let it lie and create a good feeling in the customer. The dance is always driven by the customer. Let him or her call all the shots, and you will be danced into more business!

Referral Call

If this is a referral call, generated by a customer, internal contact, friend, or through networking, begin your call using the referral name. Your call might sound like this:

Salesperson: Robert, Hello, this is _____ from _____ company. Mac MacDonald suggested I call you about your interest in streamlining your purchasing.

Cold Call

In a true cold call, your opener should include a reference to the customer's company. For example, it might sound like this:

Salesperson: Ms. Denos, this is _____ from _____. I read in this week's *Wall Street Journal* that your company is preparing a rollout of _____. I'd like to speak with you regarding how we can assist you with your _____.

Remember that most people enjoy talking about themselves or their company, especially if there is something particularly good to be proud of. Monitor your local business news publication (most larger cities have these) and/or the business news section of your local paper or use an online news source. Look for any changes in management, new product announcements, or contract awards. Sending a copy of the article with a note would be an excellent reason to call as a follow-up. Remember, the more you demonstrate what you already know about the company, the more anything you have to say will sound like helpful information from a concerned source.

Another possible opener might be:

Salesperson: Ms. Denos, this is _____ from _____. Your company recently acquired XYZ, and I'm calling to discuss how we can save you time during the transition.

Remember to know enough about the company that the only "cold" element in your call is the fact that you have not spoken with that person before. When you know the company's business and competitors and the customer's news, it will be easy for you to come up with the appropriate opening benefit statement. You need to strike a nerve in the first few seconds; you can't count on the prospect politely waiting for you to go down a laundry list of features until one gains attention. Even if you have not had the opportunity to uncover articles or news about the company, you can certainly learn about the challenges that companies in that category have. That information will allow you to gain interest immediately and establish credibility quickly.

Persistent or Pest?

How do you know if you are annoying the customer by calling too much? Two sets of guidelines that follow will help you in deciding this important question. Personality considerations play a big part in determining how much calling is necessary. Also, the degree to which your customer wants to be available has an impact.

Personality

If your customer is an **Assured,** you might need to leave twenty messages to get her attention. Ask yourself these questions and be honest: How urgent is the call? What is your time frame? Is this a regular customer? Do we have a good or bad relationship? What else might be going on in this customer's life that affects her returning my calls?

An **Energized** customer needs to be reminded that you are still there and trying to contact him. He needs the reminder, since he is the least organized of the four personalities. Make sure you use lots of energy in your voice and a sense of urgency in your call. Resist the urge to use words like *emergency*, because that's deceptive. Just be friendly, fun, and keep calling until you finally reach him.

For the more passive customers (**P**s and **K**s), you probably should space out your calls, so as not to pester the customers. Since these people are more introverted, they don't want to be overly pressured in your calls. A good phrase to use with these customers is "at your convenience."

Regardless of personality style, persistence sometimes involves moving your calling effort to the contact's cell phone. You can avoid being considered a pest, if you respect certain guidelines for cell phone communication.

Cellular Phone Boundaries

More and more customers are leaving their cell phone numbers on outgoing voice mail and on their business cards. There is definitely a right and a wrong way where mobile phones are concerned. Just because customers leave their cellular number on voice mail, this doesn't mean that *you* necessarily have permission to call. Most of your customers are leaving their mobile number on voice mail so that *their* customers and coworkers can get in touch with them. That's not an invitation for the rest of us to call those closely held numbers.

On voice mail, customers don't say, "Here is my mobile number, but if you are selling, don't call." But you might do well to think of it this way: *If you do not already have a relationship with the customer, then you're spamming the customer's mobile line.* Also, most people who depend on their mobile phones answer them wherever and whenever—often at inappropriate times—which is not in your best interest. Both of these scenarios will set you up for first-impression failure. Besides, it never hurts to lean toward the courteous route.

For general guidelines, it is okay to call customers on their cell phone *only if:*

▲ You have a relationship with the customer and you haven't reached the person after multiple tries on the work line.

▲ You have left multiple messages (at least five over a period of time), and the customer has not returned your call.

▲ Your customer has invited you to call her cell phone and has expressed that this is the preferred method of getting in touch with her.

If you have determined, though, that it is strategically appropriate to call a customer's mobile phone, remember that you are interrupting something she is doing: attending a meeting, cheering at a child's ball game, leaving the doctor's office—and most certainly is not anticipating your call. You have inserted yourself into the customer's work or personal life. For this reason, unless you have a well-prepared opening line, you are more than likely going to be shut down by the customer in that call.

For more detailed guidance, look at the following situations:

▲ *Call with Prior Relationship.* When you reach the customer, say, "Melissa, you know I don't like to call you on your cell phone, but I really need to talk with you about the order. Do you have just a moment?" Be sure to wait for her answer on this, or you have lost the good impression advantage. Melissa will reschedule or have a conversation with you *if you ask first*. With such respectful treatment from you, she will probably apologize for not having returned your previous calls.

▲ ***Call with No Prior Relationship.*** "Hello Joe, this is _____ (your name). I know you've been very busy, and I needed to get in touch with you about your advertising this year." After the opener, don't ask Joe if he has time to talk. See how it goes. He may agree, reschedule, or reject. Keep in mind that you must have made multiple good-faith efforts to reach Joe through his work line. He knows this, too, since you've already left him multiple messages on his office voice mail.

Last, resist the urge to leave messages on customers' mobile phones, unless you have a good relationship with them. Otherwise, you're at risk of alienating the customer by sounding like a potential stalker.

In general, it is best to take a conservative approach on the use of mobile phones, because the likelihood of success is far greater on a landline than on wireless service.

The Payoff

Everyone likes a sure thing. However, success is never a sure thing. This realization sometimes makes telephone salespeople hesitate or procrastinate when it is time to begin calling. The skills you have gained in this chapter will improve the odds of success, without doubt—*if you use them!* Planning, setting appointments, and ensuring your customers are available and "up for" your call appointments will improve your contact rate and, ultimately, your close rate and income.

CHAPTER 7

Listening Through
the Words

DO YOU REMEMBER singing in a group? Maybe it was at church or camp; possibly it occurred with a group of friends and a guitar in a dorm room in college. And there were always several kinds of singers. You remember, there was the guy who sang horribly but was the only one who always knew the words. The one who played the guitar could sing well—as long as the music was in the C key. One had an amazing voice and stood out above all the others, never missing a note and dominating the sound. And then there was the final one, the person everyone wanted to hear. With her keen ear for music and her amazing talent, she used her voice to blend with the others, making everyone sound better. This person's listening ability, skill, and melodic use of her voice made her the most effective in the group.

A good salesperson—no, the *best* salespeople—can pick up on layers of customer needs, customer personality types, possible objections, and the timing of a close, all on the phone, and all by listening intently. Admittedly, this is a two-part process: focusing sharply enough to catch all the subtle as well as the direct messages the customer sends *and* then processing those messages into the best strategy to close the sale. The first and most necessary step, however, is *strategic* listening at a deeper level.

As a salesperson, you are under pressure to make decisions very quickly about whether to pursue a call or cut your losses and contact a better prospect. This pressure can potentially eliminate sales. A professional consultative salesperson accepts the challenge and capitalizes on the unique situation every conversation presents. Listening strategically over the phone is as essential as being able to talk.

As you are listening, you should be asking yourself some of the following questions:

▲ Is this customer receptive?

▲ Is this customer too busy to talk?

▲ Does this customer sound stressed?

▲ Is this customer multitasking during your call?

▲ Does this customer sound happy you called?

▲ What is the personality type of the customer?

You need to immediately pick up on your customer's energy that comes through the phone. Even on a customer-requested follow-up call, which should be an easy path to a close, you want to be alert. A lack of enthusiasm in the customer's tone can mean any number of things. You'll want to uncover whether this lackluster manner is because of changed conditions concerning the sale or just a change in mood that has nothing to do with you or your product. If conditions have changed, your job is to regroup quickly and strategize for a new goal. For example, you may decide to set an appointment for a later time when the customer might be more receptive and less distracted.

Also, keep in mind that the customer's job is to get you off the phone as quickly as possible without your making a sale. That's part of the game of phone selling. Nowhere in the customer's job description is the phrase "entertain calls from salespeople." That's too bad. The reality is customers have become so accustomed to salespeople who unprofessionally waste their time by telling, telling, and more TELLING, that they think we *all* talk too much. Regardless of what businesses those other salespeople represent, they are competing for your customer's time. So, that's your *real* competition: time. Your attention to the customer, demonstrated by your listening, can be a differentiator. Are your competitors listening at the same level that you are? Believe me, your customer knows—and votes with his or her dollars.

Personality Style Listening

In your first call, listen for the customer's personality style. This is called *strategic listening* in which you pass from casual listening in its intensity and purpose to a deeper level. You have only two to three seconds in effective conversation time to react and choose a strategy suitable to a personality type, and you must be very quick in your choice of response. The information you gain from this type of listening will determine what you choose to say or do next. You can blow the deal if you try to close when the customer has in some way indicated that the best choice is to ask for an appointment for a later conversation.

K—These customers come off as calm and friendly. When you read the tones, your strategy might be to say something supportive instead of probing. Listen for hesitation or uncertainty. Since these customers aren't comfortable saying no outright, you must listen for more subtle cues. **K**s know that they often get taken advantage of, so as they become more business savvy, they also become more cautious. This caution is reflected in their slow and deliberate decision-making style. Words that **K**s might use are:

Teamwork	Careful	Unhurried
Collaboration	Considering	Referrals

P—These customers tend to sound monotone and speak more slowly, pause often, and hide their emotions. So, you must avoid interrupting even if their answers are maddeningly slow. You need to pause more frequently to allow them to give you something to work with. Listen to the **P**'s carefully chosen words. Concentrate on the detail clues they are providing you in the call.

You will hear **P**s say words such as:

| Cautious | Results | Detailed |
| Proven | Benchmark | Statistics |

E—These customers sound more emotional and hurried whether the situation warrants that response or not. They interrupt and are generally talkative and opinionated. You must listen as energetically as they talk, by asking lots of "tell me" questions. They will volunteer most of what you want to know. Listen carefully for their inflection—these customers emphasize their real needs. Since these customers create as they go, allow them to talk and you will end up learning what you need to know to close the sale.

Words you will hear **E**s say include:

| Excited | Glowing | Everyone |
| Relationship | Exceptional | Unbelievable |

A—These customers sound direct, impatient, and hurried. This type of customer knows what he wants and will tell you, usually in an abrupt manner. You'll want to listen to his real needs, and focus your brief presentation on his specific goal. Be prepared to listen, process, and respond quickly or you will find yourself at the other end of a dial tone.

Words you will hear **A**s say in your calls include:

| Bottom line | End game | ROI |
| Results | Profitability | Opportunity |

The Listening Challenge

Paying attention to why we, as salespeople, too often fall short of the most effectual listening can help us to turn this shortcoming into a strength. Listening is both a skill and an asset.

Sadly, all too often, we don't listen well because of some of the following reasons:

- ▲ We have never formally been taught listening as a skill.
- ▲ We have short attention spans.
- ▲ We multitask while on the phone.
- ▲ We begin to steamroll in our enthusiasm.
- ▲ We are so intent on our next question or comment that we disregard the customer's reaction.

Sound familiar? Now think back to school. (Okay, that may not be a happy thought necessarily, but go with it here for just a moment.) You had courses in reading and writing, history and math, but do you remember taking any listening classes? Most people haven't had any. And by the way, do you remember receiving any financial reward for listening to what your teachers said?

That interval in your young life might have caused you to grow up with more listening avoidance skills than listening enhancements. You may have even developed distaste for listening purposefully for a long period of time to anyone who isn't really interesting to you. And we all know that not every customer is interesting to us!

Now, fast-forward to the sales challenges you face every day. Today, years removed from the classroom, the greatest tool you have for your success is the ability to listen to your customer. Let's assess the situation this puts you in: You have never had a serious listening course, and the biggest skill you need to be successful in your job is listening!

Becoming a *strategic listener* is a necessity *now*. To do this, you need to overcome two major challenges:

1. **Obstacle Challenges.** These are challenges that can inhibit efficient listening and cause you to lose sales, such as multitasking distractions, inability to see customer reactions, restlessness, and fatigue.

2. **Attitude Challenges.** Most of us are generally more interested in what we have to say than in what others have to say. We wait impatiently for our chance to speak, especially when we have something else to say and are enthusiastic about the topic.

Both these types of challenges have several elements to them and can be handled easily with a little self-management.

Obstacle Challenges

An obstacle is something in the way of our listening success. Whether you eliminate obstacles or merely find a way around them, one thing is certain: You cannot afford to ignore them.

Multitasking Distractions

Part of what attracts many of us to the sales profession (besides the *money!*) is that it is a fast-paced, varied, and challenging career. For this reason, we often find ourselves multitasking—for example, using our computer to e-mail prospects, filling out an expense report while on the phone, placing a sandwich order with a colleague, and making coffee at our desk. Sometimes we get a misguided impression that by multitasking, we are getting more done. Let's take a closer look at this belief.

On the phone, multitasking can be the kiss of death, because if our attention is divided, we are not listening to our customers! When we stop listening, we miss important details that might lead to a sale. When we check e-mail, review our stock portfolio, mouth silent conversations with colleagues, and engage in other activities, our heads are down, and our tone and inflection are impaired. Even rocking in your seat will make you sound different to a customer and affect your ability to listen to the subtleties in the call. In addition, these subtle changes in your tone and inflection are heard by the customer on the other end, thereby impeding your ability to gain a rapid rapport.

Self-Management Solution The real sales professional organizes and prepares for sales calls. Don't pick up the phone until you have done the following:

▲ Cleared your desk

▲ Turned your chair away from all distractions

▲ Closed your door, or put out a MAKING CALLS—PLEASE DO NOT DISTURB sign

▲ Turned off audible distractions such as music, alert tone on e-mail, and your call waiting

▲ Prepared yourself to make and/or take calls

Your job for that interval is to listen to your customer. Those who listen build better relationships, know more about customer needs, and close more business.

The only exception is writing down what the customer is saying. Capturing customer's keywords are an important way to track what your customer is thinking. Writing is a good way to keep you focused, and the notes are helpful long after you have finished the call. Lastly, you now have a written record of the conversation that you can refer to later, enter into your contact manager, and use for preparing a customer-centered proposal.

Inability to See Customer Reaction

In face-to-face sales exchanges, part of our "listening" is watching visual cues. Experts tell us that we read lips, draw conclusions about people by their clothing, and interpret mood or predisposition by body language, fidgeting, and facial expression. On the phone, we have none of these clues. We have to determine where our customers are in their thinking with only words and tone.

For example, there are many messages in the nonwords part of communication that can give us a direct line to a close. Does the person sound hurried? Hesitant? Are there many pauses or are you hearing enthusiasm and fast tempo? Does the person sound friendly, engaging, or irritated that he or she has been interrupted? What information can you gather about customers from the *way* they speak? A great deal can be learned from tone and tempo, but you need to listen purposefully beyond the words themselves.

Tone Clues—Emphasis

"I am NOT the decision-maker." (possibly wants to get you out of their face)

(continues)

"I am not THE decision maker." (Suggests there might be a team or group decision)

"I am not the DECISION MAKER." (Tricky. This may suggest that, though not the actual decision maker, this person may have a significant part to play anyway.)

"I am not (pause) the decision maker." (Sounds like they may be involved in the decision but there are others and he knows who they are.)

"You've caught me at a bad time." (If this is said friendly and quickly, the person may be interested but it's truly a bad time. Ask for an appointment.)

Now, you practice with someone and figure out what each means:

Read aloud: "We are not really purchasing at this time." Read it four times, emphasizing a different word to note the differences in meaning.

We are not REALLY purchasing at this time.
We are NOT really purchasing at this time.
We are not really PURCHASING at this time.
We are not really purchasing AT THIS TIME.

Self-Management Solution Use the personality types as a template. Once you have determined what type your customer is, you will be able to compare what you are hearing on the phone to the predictable behavior of that type. Here again, keeping some short notes will help, especially if you have many different customers.

For example, you have a customer who is a **Precise**. **Precise** people experience stress when pushed to act quickly without sufficient information. Remember, these customers are into detail, facts, and correctness. A conversation could go like this: (In the prior call, the customer had asked many detailed questions and shown great interest. This was a callback at his request.)

Precise: Hello.

Salesperson: Hello, Leo. This is Josh from Amalgamated Services; you wanted me to get back with you about—

Precise (interrupts): Yeah, well Josh, it's a busy day today, I really don't have time—

Salesperson: Leo, it sounds like you're really under the gun. Is there anything I can do to help right now?

Precise (with a more pleasant tone): You got that right. My manager wants everything yesterday and we're still studying the situation. We're going to have to carefully set up a process in order to make sure the production schedule goes just right.

Salesperson: I'm sure as a project manager you have to pay attention to everything the other guys don't even think of. You know, we've got a systems guy that just came off a half-million-dollar project, similar to what your company has been working on. He could come on a short contract to help get you over the hump. Would that help?

Precise: At this point, we are prepared to consider options; there's just too much for me to keep up with. Send over a proposal; I want to know all the particulars before I go to my manager with it.

This clever salesperson turned an attempted brush-off into a possible sale.

> **Tip** Tuning in to the *entire* message takes you where your customer is, and active listening is such a rare behavior in business conversation these days that the surprise value alone may get the customer's attention.

Short Attention Span—Restlessness

Many people in sales tend to be right-brain dominant and, quite frankly, often a little on the high energy side. These are great assets in our business, but they can cause us to have a short attention span for ideas coming in from the outside. We get bored during the call when the customer is talking, especially if the customer is rambling.

This really isn't surprising, considering that people only talk at about 250 words per minute, and the brain can process at more than 1,000 words per minute (look at speed readers). Eventually, our high-speed brains drive us to start looking around for something entertaining. Unfortunately, when we do that, we become redirected. Mentally zoning out can cause us to miss an important element in the conversation, an element that might determine the sale.

Self-Management Solution If you find yourself mentally checking out, you can try the following:

▲ Doodling—which engages the right hemisphere of your brain.

▲ Playing with a squeeze ball (left hand to engage right brain).

▲ Walking around your space. (You may be someone who thinks better when you are moving. You know the expression, "I think better on my feet." It's because your blood is moving through your body. You're getting more oxygen to your brain. Also, when walking around, you can move your arms more freely and this produces a better tonal emphasis in your calls.)

▲ Do not multitask (except as recommended previously), regardless of the temptation to do so. Your customers will know it!

Here is a skill practice activity that can help you to improve your focus:

Exercise: When you are on your next call, put a pen and pad by the phone. During the conversation, every time you recognize that you have drifted away from your customer focus, put a mark on the pad. At the end of the call, note how many marks you have and make a mental note to try for fewer the next time. You may be surprised how often you have gotten off track during a call, when you thought you were generally paying attention. Keep practicing until you can stay with the customer for ten full minutes at a time.

Attitude Challenges

Everyone has heard the term *attitude adjustment*. One important aspect of our degree of willingness to listen is the value we place on time; another is the value we place on what the other person has to say relative to what we want to say. These two factors are attitude issues and are dealt with next.

Impatience—Time Perception

A much-quoted study by the American Medical Association showed that American doctors give patients about twenty-three seconds to relate their symptoms and concerns before jumping in. That same study, though, found that most patients, when allowed to finish, speak for an average of only twenty-nine seconds. The difficulty is an impatient person's perception of time. The doctors thought they would fall behind with their appointments if they let patients rattle on endlessly. Apparently, their worries were unwarranted.

Also, those of us with really high-speed thinking may be less aware of exactly how much time has passed during our conversations with customers. Try the exercise below to see how your impression of time passage compares with actual duration.

Exercise: Gauging the passage of time— one minute

1. Use a stopwatch, if possible, or a clock with a digital number counter.
2. Note a start time, then turn your back on the watch or clock.
3. When you think one minute has passed, press the stopwatch button or turn around to view the clock.

Results?

Just a guess, but you probably stopped the clock long before a minute was up.

As long as the customer is talking, your chances of getting the sale go up. The reverse is true, also. As long as you are talking, the customer's interest is probably down. Although one of our greatest assets as sales professionals is our willingness to communicate, sadly, one of our detriments is that we tend to talk too much. This liability is exaggerated on the phone, because we are not able to read if the customer is "with us" or not. So, we often keep talking in hopes of keeping the customer engaged. In fact, the customer probably has a short attention span as well and is probably not engaged when we are going on and on and on. To the customer *we* sound like we talk too much.

Self-Management Solution Use the "tongue trick." When you are tempted to interrupt, take your tongue and place it behind your teeth. That is a gentle physical reminder to be quiet until the customer is finished. (You can use this technique in face-to-face interactions, as well, and no one is the wiser.) This will help you to abide by our 80/20 rule: The customer should be talking 80 percent of the time. While the customer is talking, remember that you should be really listening, not just waiting for your turn to talk. You should be speaking only 20 percent. So, with this guideline, *do you* talk too much?

You are probably not timed on how long you are on the phone. That could be disastrous to your selling credibility. If you are, then you'll want to best organize your call to still adhere to the 80/20 rule, which is especially effective for **E**s and **A**s, who really want to run the conversation. **P**s and **K**s are better listeners, so you may alter those proportions for them, but be careful. **P**s and **K**s need better conversational questioning to follow this rule.

Steamrolling—Features Enthusiasm

As salespeople representing products or services we believe in, we sometimes get wrapped around our knowledge. We are so excited about what we sell and so intent on what we want to say, that we feel like we have to throw out every neat feature and include a cherry on top! Let's face it, we begin to enjoy our captive audience because we all like people to listen to us.

For example, a sales rep who has just come through a lengthy new product training course would want to share her knowledge, especially if it is truly a super innovation. Any good salesperson is a subject matter expert, and it makes sense that you are eager to convey all you've learned. Unfortunately, the customer may need only a tiny piece of what you know. The customer *only* wants his or her problem solution—not an encyclopedia of *all* you know.

As a sales presentation trainer, I constantly hear justifications from salespeople for the fifty-two-slide PowerPoint presentation. Their argument for these mind-numbing ordeals is "But I have to cover all this material." No offense to college classes, but does anyone out of school want to sit through that? Even if the customer is interested at the beginning, the fatigue of looking at a screen for that long would kill any interest. Our verbal flood on the phone can have the same numbing effect on our customers.

Now, ask yourself this tough question: Is talking more helping you close more sales? If it is, you are in the minority.

Let's take a look at this example to emphasize the point: You are calling a decision maker about purchasing replacement cartridges for printers. Your immediate goal might be selling a gross of printer cartridges. If you are so focused on getting out all you had to say, you may miss a casual comment from the customer about replacing all the copiers. In your zeal to "tell," you missed an opportunity to sell.

Self-Management Solution Remember the doctors who interrupted in the previous section? Your customers are no different. When you have talked longer than thirty seconds at a stretch, they think you have talked too much—*unless* you are specifically addressing their needs, which you will only discover by *listening*!

Put a silent timer near the phone. (One of those minute timers that looks like a small hourglass is great; you can sometimes find them at yard sales in old board games that people are getting rid of, or at a dollar store.) Just for fun, you can time your customer as he or she talks. For self-management development, time yourself and let the timer help you regulate your talk time. When the sand runs low, ask the customer a check-in question, such as: "How does that sound to you, Fred?" or a closing question, such as: "Tell me your thoughts on that feature for your business."

Disinterest in Other People

Another attitude element is our own disinterest in other people. If customers on the other end are boring or don't talk openly, we may feel the need to talk more to keep the conversation going. Why, then, are they boring to us? We may think that what we have to say is *much* more interesting than what they have to say. It could be because we have not asked enough pertinent questions. The prospect may have even said no earlier, and because we didn't listen and kept going, has zoned out, is multitasking, or is waiting for a pause to break in and hang up.

Some of us are genuinely curious about people and their individual story. Others see people as merely a means to an end. Whatever your own basic attitude is, it probably comes through in your phone manner.

Self-Management Solution First of all, using personality matching to help you strategize should make every customer interaction more interesting. A prospect becomes a puzzle that you complete by uncovering clues within the conversations that you engineer. It is *your* job to find what is interesting about the customer. Take the three most boring customers or prospects you have and apply the personality matching techniques to your next conversation. You might find that the issue is a personality-style difference between you two and that by using the strategies in this book, you can turn boredom into bucks!

The Payoff

Good listening takes the focus off the "me" (the salesperson) and puts it on the "you"(the customer). For some of us that can be hard to do, especially when we are enthusiastic about our product or when we are very goal-driven. And, good listening can be exhausting; actively hearing and processing information while strategizing the next level of the conversation takes a lot of energy. For this reason, occasional breaks in your call day will help. What should help more, though, is remembering that the reason for listening is for *you* to *make the sale to anyone over the phone.*

Asking High-Value Questions

IN THE MUSICAL *Fiddler on the Roof*, there is a lovely question-and-answer duet. It is an exchange between an older man and his wife, deciding the question, "Do you love me?" Not only are the words a question-and-answer dialog, but the music also has an easily discernable query-response sound. Too often, though, our questioning in our sales calls comes across more like "Dueling Banjos"; a series of challenges where one attempts to outdo another. In a duet, like the one from the musical mentioned here, the two singers soon stop the back-and-forth of separate lines and begin to sing together. They harmonize in perfectly blended voices as they duplicate each other's words. This is the point you want to get to in your sales calls—harmony and a joining of purpose, which leads to the sale.

The Relationship

In a conversational sales approach you, as the sales professional and product expert for your company, begin by gathering information and establishing, or deepening, the relationship with your customer. Customers don't like the feeling of being interrogated or being "sold." Customers like to *buy*. And that's okay because you aren't selling in the old, strong-arm way. You are building a relationship based on mutual respect and conversing with a customer whose busi-

ness or bottom line will be enhanced by a product you have. You just
need to find out how that will work.

Not Personal

What has been traditionally taught and what worked in the old days,
for example, was asking personal questions to build rapport at the
outset of the sales call. Today, this kind of chitchat sounds amateur-
ish; it also jeopardizes the business relationship early on by wasting
the customer's valuable time. Today's busy customers rarely spend
time with their closest loved ones, so they don't typically welcome
making new friends over the phone. Why would you think a person
would welcome being interrupted from the demands of a *business* day
for a *non*-business-sounding call?

Customers may resent being pulled into a personal conversation
at work and with strangers, but they *will* pay attention to information
and questions about their business. You can become an integral part
of the success of their business, but they don't necessarily want to be
involved with you personally. That's why you can't take this personally. A solid business relationship is all you need, and all that your
customers want until you've reached an appropriate point in your
relationship.

That is not to say that a business → personal relationship never
occurs. Many of us likely have personal friends we met through work.
(In fact, the two authors of this book first met professionally, then
developed a personal and business relationship.) But if it does, it will
grow naturally with people to whom we are attracted; it will not be
created by artificial plays at friendship with customers.

Use your business tone of voice as the *real* opener, so that every
question is in a conversational, professional tone. A warm opening is
followed by a cogent question in a businesslike tone, instead of saying, "Hi, how's the wife and kids?" We even want to avoid, "How
are you today?" (The reasoning for avoiding this latter question will
be explained later in the chapter.)

Not Transactional

On the other hand, the sales conversation is not merely a transaction
either. Transactional selling says, "I've got a product; you've got $5,

there it is." This is why we avoid questions like, "Are you the decision maker?" or "Do you have a $50,000 budget?"

As openers these two questions rarely earn you the chance to complete the call or to get a return call back. They aren't relationship-building questions. In transactional selling, the situation is clearly about you and what you want. Customers get enough of that treatment from their own bosses and from other steamroller salespeople. Questions that make it clear that you are, instead, interested in what the customer might want will take you a long way toward the close.

Every contact with a customer is a relationship. Whether it's a one-call close or long-term business, some form of relationship must exist for you to make a sale. If you want sustained sales, the relationship must be positive. If you are in sync with your customer, you are questioning and learning, then becoming part of the input for the purchase decision. This makes you a *partner*. Customers will rely on you for information; and you can rely on them for sales closed over the phone.

Questions Qualify

Let's take a slightly different look at the qualifying portion of the sales call. If you fail to qualify well, you dramatically reduce your ability to close. In qualifying, you begin the process of guiding the customer to making his or her own buying decision. That's right. Today's customers don't want to be told what to buy. This process involves you leading the customer to make that decision through strategic qualifying questions. Even though you haven't conducted a detailed benefits presentation at this point, your goal is to gain the customer's attention by asking the right high-value questions.

In the strategic qualifying method you do the following:

▲ Establish credibility as an expert in the customer's situation

▲ Uncover your customer's real needs

▲ Deepen your customer relationships

▲ Lay out a foundation of how you are going to present your sales solutions

If you don't qualify well, you won't get the customer's attention. Remember, customers are busy and are not really thinking about buying your product when the phone rings. The way you ask the customers questions tells them if you are interested in their business and if you are listening—*really* listening.

Questions Establish Credibility

If the customer doesn't know you, your strategic qualifying will establish credibility if the questions are well thought out in advance. The presentation that follows qualifying is where you share your idea of a solution, so it's critical that your credibility is already established by that point. Qualifying must be done early and correctly because your intelligent qualifying differentiates you from other salespeople, and that's what we all want—differentiation. Without differentiation from all the others who call your customer, you won't get the sale. You achieve this in large part by just asking smart, well-thought-out questions. Remember that *smart,* as defined by your customer, means directly relevant to his or her business.

For example, a salesperson might ask:

"Tell me how you handle your wasted paper."

This is an intelligent question for someone in the newspaper or printing business because wasted paper is a concern in that industry. You have shown that you know what the customer is dealing with by asking a relevant question. Notice that we used the word *tell* to begin the qualifying, and we used second person *you* or *your* twice in one sentence.

Questions Guide the Process

Your goal is to get your customer singing off the same song sheet with you. How do you do that? The answer is by using a specific process of qualifying that builds rapport, establishes your credibility, and maximizes your opportunities for closing the sale.

Questions Uncover Needs

You uncover needs by asking questions to help lead the customer to making his or her own decision to use your product. Think of yourself as a detective. Here are some examples of questions you might ask:

- ▲ "Tell me about your existing situation."
- ▲ "What is the application (purpose/use)?"
- ▲ "Where is the installation?"
- ▲ "How is this going to be implemented?"
- ▲ "Who will be using these products?"
- ▲ "Tell me what other products you are currently using."

Sometimes your questioning can help customers uncover needs they didn't know they had. When this happens, you confirm your position as a consultant who can contribute in a meaningful way to the success of your customer's business. Thus, product or service recommendations you make after that point will be well received, and you are on your way to longer-term business. The reason is that the customer is being led down the path of buying your solution—not by your *telling* him all about your great products, but by the customer making his own decision. The added advantage of this strategy is that once customers make their own decisions, they rarely renege on a commitment.

Questions Deepen Relationships

As you are asking well-thought-out questions, your customer is most probably impressed with your ability to pin down her greatest challenge that your product will solve. In addition, your customers are used to being "talked at" by your competition regarding how great their products are. You will rise above the fray by deepening your customer relationships and asking more strategic questions. However, you need to ask the *right* questions.

Avoid the Wrong Questions

If you ask the wrong question or ask a too-personal question too soon, customers will cut you off, and you will *never get back in again.* Think of it like this: If you were to purchase a new refrigerator and the salesperson asked you how much money you had as her opening question, wouldn't you feel a bit put off?

In the qualifying stage, note that asking, "How are you?" is not a good opening question because we truly don't care, and the customer knows we don't care. In addition, the immediate message the customer gets is "Oh, no! Another inexperienced salesperson!" Further, you can open up yourself for failure from the beginning. For example, if the customer answers the "How are you?" question with "Terrible!" or ignores the question, the customer is controlling the call and your game has been thrown off. Such a routine and potentially damaging question causes you to be seen as flaky, when you want to be perceived as knowledgeable and ultimately helpful to secure the sale. *Break this habit* if you have it!

You want to ensure that each of your qualifying questions is well thought out to maximize interaction and information from your customer. When questions are too personal too quickly, customers freeze. You hear it in the hesitation on the other end, when the questions are asked at inappropriate times (usually, too soon).

If your customers freeze on a question, then consider your timing (read on for more on this). Next are the top questions you should not ask and the reasons for not asking them, even though you may have heard them from other sales sources. After the freeze question, see the better alternatives to use in sales calls.

Freeze question #1: "What do you know about us?"

This is a "me, me, me" question and assumes that knowledge of your company will make the sale. Probably not. In addition, you have put your customer on the spot. Making your customer feel uncomfortable isn't a good way to build a relationship leading to sales. Also, it sounds like a test question. No one likes those.

Alternatives to build better rapport and get a more honest answer are:

▲ "Tell me what you are currently using."

▲ "Tell me, when was the last time you purchased from our company?"

▲ "Tell me about your situation."

Freeze question #2:"What will it take to get your business?"
Asked as an early question, before needs or credibility or relationship are established, this is a sure dead end. The answer you will invariably force from the customer is, "Uh, nothing." The implied message here is that you will do *anything* to get their business. Think through the logic here, are you willing to drive to Montana and personally deliver the goods, provide free service for a year, or lower your price to less than cost? If you aren't willing to make these types of commitments, don't ask your customer this question. Also, it sounds cheesy because the customer knows it is an insincere question. At any point, even later in the call, it creates discomfort, so why use it?
    Better alternatives are:

▲ "What is your time frame for making a decision on this project?"

▲ "What else might you need to take this recommendation to your colleagues?"

▲ "How can I make your decision-making process easier?"

Freeze question #3: "How much money do you want to spend?"
For customers, the ideal for this is "nothing." Maybe this question is supposed to establish budget, but instead, it just reminds the customer that he or she is probably spending more than desired—even on something that is needed. In addition, a customer that is insulted by the question, may respond with: "None of your business." Any customer answer is misleading, because there is no buying relationship yet. Also, why would a customer tip his or her hand that early?
    Better alternatives are:

▲ "Tell me about your budget range."

▲ "What are your price expectations for this installation?"

▲ "When you purchased last time, what was the price range?"

Freeze question #4: "Who makes the decision?"
There's nothing like insulting the customer with a frontal attack. This question implies that the customer you're speaking with doesn't have the authority or the intelligence to make a decision. So, not only have you insulted your customer, you have set yourself up for failure because the insulted customer will always answer with the response: "I do." And this may or may not be true. The main problem is that you have risked alienating the customer, and the likelihood of making the sale is reduced or eliminated. You also don't know who the decision makers are.

Better alternatives are:

▲ "Tell me about your decision-making process."

▲ "What method of selecting a vendor do you use?"

▲ "How are you going to make your decision?"

How do you know what a good quality question is? If a customer is responding and offering information, then it is a good quality question. Also, if you feel that the energy on the other end of the phone is going well, then your qualifying questions are on the right track.

Guidelines for High-Value Questions

The basic concept of high-value questions referred to here is the four Ws, H, and T qualifying process.

Who, what, when, where, but *never* why. Why questions put customers on the defensive. Think of it this way: All small children ask, "Why?"—16,000 layers of "why." Also, children are chastised with, "Why did you do that?" "Why can't you get it right?" It is too often used in an accusative way. It's an annoying question, so as adults we are resistant to responding to why questions.

Good *W* questions may include:

▲ "*When* is the ideal time for implementation?"

▲ "*What* departments are involved during installation?"

▲ "*Who* is going to be using the product at your company?"

▲ "*Where* are you planning on storing the extra stock?"

How, or *H,* questions are great for understanding a process and application.

▲ "*How* is the workload distributed?"

▲ "*How* are the two departments involved in the decision?"

▲ "*How* are these materials applied?"

▲ "*How* many do you anticipate needing in the next twelve months?"

The very best, though, are the *T* (tell) questions. After twenty years, I realize the tell questions are the most effective because asking *T* questions encourages customers to talk. (Remember, when the customer is talking, he's selling himself on *you* because you are listening, right?) When asked the right questions, customers enjoy sharing experiences, telling stories, and relating needs. Also, you will find that by asking more *T* questions, you will learn more about your customer's needs in less time. When you learn what is on the customer's mind, you are most likely to solve the customer's problem. Of course, you can't use "Tell me . . ." for every sentence, just as you wouldn't use any of the *W*s or *H* before each qualifying question. The *T* is golden because once you get in the habit of asking more of these questions, you'll find the necessity of asking too many questions—which may sound like an interrogation—eliminated. Thus, we want to ask only high-value questions.

Last, remember never to interrupt your customer after asking a question, even if the phone silence is uncomfortable. Respect your customer's communication style by being quiet after asking a question and resisting the urge to answer for the customer. Use the tongue trick to stay quiet. Just gently place your tongue behind your front teeth, which is the reminder to be quiet until the customer is finished speaking.

Your **P** and **K** customers are most likely to hesitate after hearing a question. Remember, these personality types are generally more passive and don't blurt out information quickly. They are used to being interrupted by less professional salespeople. Differentiate yourself by letting these customers process the question and respond— without *your* interrupting them!

Exercise: Make a list of as many of your qualifying questions as you use regularly. Go back and change them (if needed) to who, what, when, where, how, or tell, but *not* why.

It is not enough, however, just to get the right questions. The real test of merit for the professional salesperson is to know *when* to ask each question. A money question is necessary at some point for a sale, but asking it at the wrong time kills the relationship. Qualify— but in the *right* order.

Questions at the Right Time

The strategy of getting a customer responding and eating out of your hand is to begin with easy, broad, nonthreatening questions to put your customer at ease in the call.

Instead of asking, "When did you last finance this equipment?" try "How are you handling payments now?" Keep it simple; become more specific as you go to bring in focus. Whether your product is running shoes, insurance, building supplies, or capital equipment; whether you are dealing with a new customer or it's the fiftieth call, *the pattern is the same.* Simple to more complex qualifying strategies should be your mantra in each sales call.

Remember the pattern of easy/nonthreatening → complex/personal. What so many salespeople forget is that the questions most important to them are the most personal to the customer. For this reason, the typical salesperson jumps the gun, speaks "for" the customer, and sabotages the call. The most personal and most potentially unsettling for the customer are questions about money or time because people's values (in business and in their personal lives) are determined by how they spend their money and time. As a sales professional, whatever product or service you are selling has either a money or time (or both) component to the close.

Think of your qualifying strategy as a trust scale. The more detailed the question, the more it belongs *after* the customer has relaxed during the call. After all, customers don't want to feel like the call is an interrogation, and you don't want to feel like the interrogator!

To avoid this type of adversarial situation, ask your easy, nonthreatening questions first. Think of these as 1–3 questions.

Your mid-level questions, for example, relating to issues with existing conditions, the competition, and so forth, are considered 4–7 questions on the trust scale. These questions require that the customer is more relaxed before he or she will answer honestly.

Last, your customer's most personal or threatening questions will fall between an 8–10 on the trust scale. These questions require trust before your customer will answer candidly. Think of it like this: If you ask me how much money I have to invest, I may tell you, but I won't start out a phone call that way. I'll need to know that I can trust you before providing that level of information.

Look in the following box for examples of these questions and where they would fall on the trust scale.

1–3 low anxiety, "Tell me about your situation." This is broad and nonthreatening. Makes customer feel at ease so he or she will offer more information.

4–6 usually has to do with competition, "How have you handled —— in the past?" This gives you some frame of reference on decision-making process.

8–10 more detailed or specific relating to time and/or money. "How much did you pay the last time you had this done?" "What is your anticipated budget?" "How much have you set aside?" or "When do you want the work done on site?

The following questions are discovery questions. They qualify and establish a need or process. These will be level 1–3.

▲ "Tell me about your existing situation."

▲ "Tell me how you've handled this in the past."

▲ "Who will be using the product?"

▲ "When are you considering implementation?"

Level 4–7 questions dig a little deeper into the customer's situation.

▲ "What's worked for you using your existing supplier?"

▲ "Tell me, if you could change the current process, what would you do differently?"

▲ "Tell me about your decision-making process."

▲ "What is your decision date?"

▲ "How many copies/versions do you expect to use?"

▲ "What other solutions are you considering?"

Budget and money questions are always somewhere between 8 and 10 on your qualifying scale. They should never occur in the qualifying or discovery part of your sales conversation. Look at the following example:

▲ "You mentioned your insurance will pay part of the cost; what is your deductible?"

This is a prying question that will be received well *only* if you are already considered a partner in the relationship. If this is your first question, the customer might perceive that price is conditional on insurance. However, if the customer has already offered some specifics about his or her situation, then it is a natural question.

Exercise: Refer to the list you made earlier of your usual call questions. Now, assign a number to each one depending on the comfort or possible distress level each question might create in your customer. For example:

▲ Tell me about your goals. (3)
▲ How much money have you put aside for this? (10)

Do you need to make some adjustments in your qualifying process?

After you have reordered your qualifying questions, take the top seven, put them on a colored index card and tape them next to your phone. Now you have a valuable cheat sheet to use!

Killer Questions to Avoid

The following situations are guaranteed to stop any conversation with a customer:

▲ An 8, 9, or 10 question asked too soon: "What's your budget?" "Will you buy today?"

▲ A self-serving question or a threat: "My quota ends today, will you buy?" or "If you don't make a decision by tomorrow, you'll have to pay more since the price increase will take effect."

▲ Disaffirming questions: "Should I contact your boss?" "Who makes the decision?" The implication is that customer cannot possibly have the authority. The customer, insulted, will say, however, "I do." You have now closed off finding out who really makes the buy.

▲ Clichéd or overly restrictive questions: "Is there any reason you can't buy from me today?" "What will it take to get your business?"

▲ Stupid questions: "How much money do you have?" "If I can show you how to save 50 percent on your bill, will you make a commitment today?"

Make the customer feel "I want to buy" instead of "He's trying to sell me."

> **Sales-boosting tip:** Before you tape your question list to the wall or desk near your phone, have you checked it over for any killer questions?
>
> Delete any killer or freeze questions from your regular use list. Ask a coworker to look over your list to help you edit it.

Look at the following possible scenarios as you try to frame your planning ideas.

Inbound Call Example

A customer has called a tree service company. This inbound call might be handled appropriately with asking close questions sooner (8–10) if it is a repeat customer. Remember to use "tell" questions, however, to involve the customer in an exchange even if it is a repeat customer.

▲ "Tell me what prompted you to call." (2)

▲ "What's your time frame?" (4)

▲ "How would you like to handle this?" (6)

▲ "What else might you need while we're on your property?" (9)

▲ "Are there neighbors in your area that I should call as well?"(10)

Outbound Call Example

This time, your reconnaissance work has allowed you to address the customer from a point of strength. It's a cold call, but you know what the need is before you pick up the telephone. Thus, your goals might have to include establishing credibility more than in the prior situation. For example, you might ask one of the following questions:

▲ "One of our technicians was in your area lately and noticed several trees that might be in distress. What changes have you noticed yourself recently?" (a conversational opener) (2)

▲ "Your neighbor with the large oak trees suggested that you had concerns about the trees in the front of your property. What seems to be going on?"(3)

▲ "Tell me a bit about your situation." (2)

▲ "Since there was a storm (or disease) in your area, how would you assess the condition of the trees on your property?"(3)

▲ "With those trees that are damaged, how serious is the situation? Is there a threat to property or potential for injury?"(3)

▲ "What are your expectations of what the removal is going to cost?" (10)

Before you dial this customer (assuming you have the necessary information), you should be preparing your cheat sheet of the benefits your product or service offers as they apply *directly* to this individual customer's situation. This will help you to form relevant questions, such as the following:

▲ "What may have contributed to the condition of the tree?"(3)

▲ "How long has the tree been in distress? What is the current condition?"(4)

▲ "What have you done to treat the tree?" (6)

▲ "Have you thought about doing A or B?" (Establish credibility while letting customer make decision.) (7)

▲ "When did you call your county extension service about information on this distressed tree?"(6)

▲ "Tell me, what is your time frame for having this tree evaluated?"(7)

In the next situation that follows next, you are making a cold call because you are aware of a likely weakness or problem that the customer may not readily perceive. (*Note:* You might find this scenario in technical selling situations where there isn't a technical expert within the company and you actually know more than the customer about his or her situation.) If this is the case, you need to be prepared to demonstrate knowledge of the customer's operations in a very detailed and expert way, likely in the qualifying. Remember, customers are not expecting your call and may not be prepared to answer questions about the situation.

▲ "Tell me about the overall health of the trees on your property." (3)

▲ "How has the condition of your trees changed since they were planted?" (4)

▲ "What concerns do you have about the trees on your property?" (5)

▲ "Tell me, what role do the trees play in the overall appearance of your property?" (2)

▲ "What regular maintenance do you conduct to ensure the health of your trees?" (6)

(Note this last question. Although it should be an easy one to answer, it may make the customer uncomfortable if nothing has been done. After you have established a trusting relationship with this customer, this question would not be threatening. Asked too early, it could stop the conversation.)

▲ "Who planted the trees on your property?" (5)

▲ "When were they planted?" (5)

▲ "Who selected the varieties of trees?" (6)

▲ "Tell me your expectations of a tree health maintenance service?" (7)

▲ "Should you decide to select a tree service, what would be your basis of selection?"(9)

Questions for Personality Styles

Precise—**P**s respond to questions monosyllabically. They give limited information in a monotone voice without elaboration. Seven questions from you might elicit only twenty-four words. Ask process/procedural and fact questions. This person, you can be certain, will know the number of stations that will need the software, procedures and time for the decision, users and the levels of expertise, and more.

Kind—Ks will give you a lot of answers relating to the people around them. You can ask them the following type of questions: "Tell me about what your team has been looking at so far." "Share with me how the people in your organization see these products." "How will upgrading your software affect the worker's time?" "What training might your employees need once you implement a new product?" "How can we help you with a successful installation at your office?"

Assured—As will give you the same number of words, but will be more emphatic. They are interested in their goals and like to have their authority recognized. "When do you expect to make this decision?" (authority) "Tell me about what you need this software to do?" "What do you need to accomplish with this new system?" "When are you planning on making the decision to move forward?" (goals)

Energized—Es will be thinking about self and effect on self. These customers want to talk more. "How important to you is ease of use?" "How quickly do you need this to be implemented?" "How do we make this easier for you?" "Tell me your impressions of being first in your city to have this product." Warm up to qualify.

Sometimes an **Assured** or an **Energized** will hit you with a question first. You need to take control and return to questioning yourself. For example, the customer may say: "So, what do you have that's new today?" or "Just tell me about your specials" or "What do you need?" (on a return call).

Answer by first putting a smile in your voice so that you sound friendly. This is a very important point because it allows you to control the tone of the message. "I'm happy to tell you what we have. But do you mind if I ask you a *couple* of *quick* questions first?" Emphasize the words *couple* and *quick,* so they know it's not a lengthy process. Then take control of the call by asking a question such as: "What's changed since our last conversation?"

Although there might be some variation in what each type of customer considers a 1 or a 9 question, you still need to remember that a continuum is necessary, because customers are not prepared to answer a 9 question without a warm-up.

> **Sales-boosting tip:** Remember that whatever personality type you are, you will tend to ask questions that reflect your customer's natural style.
>
> Revise your call questions list to include at least four questions for each personality type. Pay specific attention to your choices for the personality types that are different from yours. Make sure you have a good variety of "tell" questions included.

The Payoff

Notice how all these questions accomplish three important goals: they help you gather information about a customer's situation, they establish a more trusting relationship between you and your customer, and they also guide the customer's thinking toward the direction of your service. They are low-key, noninvasive, and will set the stage nicely for the next step in the process: your customized presentation.

Remember that attempts to rush the process by attempting level 9 or 10 questions too early will not get you to the close more quickly. In fact, the opposite will more likely happen, and worse, you may not be received well on later, follow-up calls. You can increase your close percentage by turning more calls into sales by respecting the customer's need for process.

Selling Through Objections

IN EVERY SALESPERSON'S DAY, there is that moment of celebration. Sometimes it is a quiet moment, when you first recognize
the customer is indeed going to buy. Sometimes it is loud cheering
and doing the "happy dance" around your office after you have hung
up the phone from closing a career-defining account. Whichever you
are experiencing, the process that took you there probably went
much like a well-crafted symphony. Each symphony has an invitation
or introduction part. Next, the music rises and falls with the flow of
the musical story. Moments of tension alternate with soothing pas-
sages. At times, the instruments may seem to veer away from the melody temporarily, yet the composer's genius always masterfully brings
harmony back by the ending.

   The sales process moves much the same way when it is properly
crafted and directed by the conductor—you. Although customers are
rarely passive and easily led to your preferred resolution, all elements
of the sales process, including obstacles, can be brought under your
control. Just as a professional musician analyzes a piece, figures out
the more difficult parts, and practices accordingly, you will be able to
"play" through the objections and end up on the right note to close
more sales.

Value of Objections

Although no one likes customer objections, in phone sales you have a big advantage: You can gather your thoughts and have a cheat sheet available to assist you with the tough ones. Another advantage of dealing with objections over the phone is that if you have a tendency to appear nervous—for example, perspire, shake, twitch, or shift in your seat—unless these natural responses come through in your voice as anxiety, you are prepared to deal with the customer, and he or she won't even know you are nervous—if indeed, you are. Last, sometimes it's easier to formulate a response when you aren't looking directly into a customer's eyes. You also get an extra second or two to think of an appropriate strategy for handling the situation.

Every time I do a sales training seminar, I ask the participants, "Do you want objections or not?" After I ask that question, there is usually silence—sometimes even a groan—reflecting the dread most feel over that part of the sale. These people obviously do not know the value of an objection.

Think of an objection as an obstacle, that's all, just a hurdle that must be navigated before moving on. And, like an athlete, when you navigate skillfully through the obstacle, you come closer to winning.

So, what should come from that room full of professional salespeople is a resounding, "Yes!" An objection should be sweet music to your ears because it tells you the customer is still paying attention *and* the sales call is still alive. Now, you have the opportunity to make a sale. If the customer isn't asking questions or objecting, he or she has checked out of the call. And, as you know, when the customer checks out, your sale is *dead*.

The following ways can alert you that the customer has mentally checked out of the call:

- ▲ Do you hear the customer typing in the background?
- ▲ Does the customer sound like his or her head is down?
- ▲ If you ask, "How does that sound to you?" the customer says "uhm" or "uh" or "I'm not sure."
- ▲ The customer pauses too long after you ask a question.
- ▲ The customer says something like, "OK, well I've heard all I need to hear."

▲ You hear, "Please repeat the question."

▲ The customer just sounds distracted with something else.

Any of these situations means that the customer wasn't listening. When this happens, you need to wake up the customer's attention again. You get an opportunity to sell at a deeper level to the customer's real needs when a question or objection occurs.

Ideally, customers pay full attention, focus completely on your presentation, and say, "Sounds good to me—let's close the deal." That perfect scenario is rare, but an objection is a beacon, a signal that the customer is indeed engaged in conversation and interested in what you are trying to convey. Note the situation here:

Salesperson: Are you ready to take delivery?

Customer: I'm not going to do something that quickly unless you handle shipping charges.

The customer's response shows that she is ready to buy or negotiate. It's a signal that value is established, and you are just working out the details.

Not quite ready to say "hooray" when an objection comes yet? What is your objection then? Is it fear that the customer will ask you something you don't know the answer to? Are you afraid he will attack you on behalf of your company for some past error? Do you worry that he might know more than you do? Well, as the song says, "don't worry, be happy," because the tips you are learning here will help you turn worry (and whining!) into *winning*.

Never Let Them "Hear" You Sweat

An old deodorant commercial showed a person who was nervously anticipating a presentation he had to conduct. When it came time to do the presentation, he didn't sweat, because (according to the advertisement) his deodorant worked. If all day you hear, "Your price is too high" or "I've never heard of your company," you may become nervous, anticipating this response from your customers. Think about it; if you react negatively or defensively, you validate the customer's perception that there is a reason not to buy. Stay cool. Handle the objection skillfully.

Remember, you are on the phone, so the customer can't see you. Never let the customer feel that you are rattled by any objection. Stay calm, cool, collected, or at least always *appear* that way to the customer through your relaxed and professional tone. If you do become uncomfortable, it won't show over the phone if you control your voice. To do this:

▲ Massage your neck to loosen tight vocal chords.

▲ Take a slow, deep breath to reduce your heart rate.

▲ Slow your rate of speech slightly, so you do not give the impression of being stressed or rushed.

▲ Stand up at your desk to allow the blood to flow better to your brain (after all, that's where the great ideas come from).

▲ And if all else fails, and you have to, simply defer the response to the objection. For example, you may have to get an okay from a higher authority and that requires getting back to the customer. However, this *is* your last resort. You may not have the opportunity to get that customer on the phone at a later time.

Of course, the best way to not appear uneasy with an objection is to *actually* not be uneasy. You come to this point by preparing, so that you:

▲ Know your customers' situations

▲ Know your product

▲ Know your competition (customers will sometimes throw that at you as an objection)

▲ Know what the objections are going to be *before* the customers state them

▲ Know how to handle any objection by thinking quickly on your feet

Knowledge is not only power; it is also confidence. We are rarely nervous in situations that are familiar and that we have navigated successfully in the past. However, we are often on edge with the unknown. So, we are going to move objections into the "known" column, and make them yet another part of the sales process over which we have control.

Be prepared and you command the situation. If the customer says, "Your price is too high," this objection should not be a surprise, because whether the product is diaper services or capital equipment, we have all heard this objection. It's almost become a standard statement. You have to be ready to respond, and that is what gives you the advantage in a phone-selling situation.

The customer doesn't know that you have heard price objections, credibility objections, or company size objections. You've heard them all and are prepared. Delivery, service, company size, credibility—none of these matters. Anticipate any objections that you regularly hear as well as any you can brainstorm and think of yourself. You'll be amazed at how much smoother you will sound during the objection-handling portion of your calls. The result? More closed sales on objections.

Objections Log Updates

It is not enough to do a one-time-only record of objections you hear. Regularly (at least once a quarter), study your list of objections and take time to think of a new and truly strategic response. Chances are, what you answered off the top of your head was not the most effective. Constantly update by adding any new information about your products or your competition to improve your answers. Practice with a coworker until you feel confident that you are on the right track to handle anything new.

If you receive objections you have never heard before (and that can always happen), read on to learn how to handle any objection in any call.

Techniques for Handling Objections

Just as you wouldn't have one outfit in your closet that takes you from a funeral to a ball game, you need a variety of different techniques to capably handle objections. Following are some ideas.

The Five-Step Technique

1. **When you first hear an objection, be quiet until the customer has completed the entire objection. Do not interrupt.** (Remember the tongue trick from Chapter 7?) It might help you to keep quiet if you jot down what the customer is saying. (Remember, you're on the phone and they can't see you.) Writing it down helps you keep a current objections database, and it ensures you have a record of what the customer said, so you can effectively counter all issues uncovered. This is especially important if you have customers who ask highly technical questions that can be potentially complicated to answer, or if the customer isn't a clear communicator.

2. **Pause at the end of the objection (count to two).** This pause says to the customer that you are thinking about his question or objection and that it is important to you. Plus, it gives you time to clarify in your own head what you think you just heard and formulate your response. You can choose what technique to use and what words will most likely lead to a close. Remember, you are in control because you knew this objection was coming. You've heard it time and time again. And if you haven't, you've just provided yourself with the opportunity of thinking over a solution.

3. **Calmly and coolly handle the objection with your well-thought-out response.** Be sure you handled *all* the concerns from Step 1. (That's why you wrote them down.) How did this person stress the objection? Did you not add enough value in your presentation portion of the call? Do you know your customer; and if so, does this person generally object as part of his or her playing out of the process? Does the objection sound like a smokescreen (a false objection)?

4. **Go for a confirmation that the objection has truly been countered.** After you feel you have satisfied the objection, ask the customer if you have resolved it for her. The reaction will let you know if you have really handled the objection. For example, you might say one of the following:

▲ "Mary, does that answer your question?"

▲ "Steve, how does that sound to you?"

▲ "Leonard, do you like that idea?"

▲ "Jackie, if I've answered your question, are you ready to sign the agreement?"

5. **If the objection is indeed handled, oftentimes this is an opportune time to a close.** Negotiation is the opportunity to sell more and can come out of an objection.

Just a piece of advice for those who still connect objection with rejection: Never take any objection personally unless the customer actually says, "I like your company and your products, it's you I don't like." (And when was the last time *that* happened?) So don't take an objection personally. It's usually not about *you*.

The Question Technique

Asking correct questions helps you to gather critically important information and to direct your customer's line of thought. We refer to this as "leading your customer down the garden path." The technique is to question so skillfully that the customer draws his or her own conclusion to buy. For example, if the customer objects, you would respond as follows:

Customer: We've used the same cleaning company in our offices for three years. We see no reason to change.

Salesperson: Oh, (brightly, then pause). James, you said you've been using the same company for three years; what initially prompted you to go with your current service when you made that decision?

You find out why they changed at that time. It could be that price, efficiency, the previous supplier went out of business, or maybe theft was an issue. Simply listen without interrupting. Hear what the customer says. Remember to listen to the tone. There are most likely a few gems of knowledge that you can gain from his response and then know where to go from there.

Then you can ask,

Salesperson: Tell me, what do you like about their service?

Customer: They use environmentally friendly chemicals. We like that.

Salesperson: How important is that to you?

Now you are in a conversation. If this aspect of James's service provider is very important, you come back with questions that uncover possible weaknesses related to that. Use a problem that you are aware of from your knowledge of your competitor's methods. For example, you know the smell of vinegar that remains after cleaning can be offensive.

Salesperson: James, what does it smell like after a treatment? (You have now raised questions in the customer's mind about the current company.)

Customer: (forced to think) Gosh, what *did* the office smell like last time? Oh, yeah, it was pretty awful. It smelled like my mother-in-law's broom closet.

You see, you didn't *tell* the customer that you know about the odor your competitors leave, even though you had that information. You, instead, let James discover it on his own through your skillful questioning. Don't tell . . . *ask*. Customers who draw conclusions on their own, while you happen to be on the phone with them, think they are pretty smart and that your timing is excellent. Customers who are *told* what the problems are may get on the defensive. For example, if you ask if the carpet stinks after the competitor leaves, the customer is most likely to respond "no" without thinking.

With the question approach, you can affirm the problem solution very easily over the phone by learning more about the customer's real needs.

Salesperson: James, what if you found a company who used environmentally safe products that didn't leave a residual smell?

That at least puts you back into the conversation.

Customer: Oh, I guess we could take a look at that. What do your chemicals smell like after a cleaning?

Salesperson: How about if we do your office for free one time and we'll see?

Customer: Sounds like a good idea. When can you come here?

Feel, Felt, Found

(*Note:* this is especially useful with **Energized** and **Kind** personality types.) This technique has been around professional selling for many years. There's a reason—it works! Just remember to mix this technique up with your other objection-handling methods during the course of your call.

Customer: I'm happy with my current supplier.

(Often, the first objection you will encounter is "we're fine like we are." This is what we refer to as the *inertia* objection.)

Salesperson: _____(customer's name). I can see why you might *feel* that way; other customers have *felt* that way before, *and* what they *found* was . . . .

Your answer must be brief and include a specific benefit to the customer. Be careful not to use the word *but;* instead, use *and*, so it doesn't sound like you are arguing with the customer. Remember that on the phone you can't soften what you say with an engaging facial expression, so your word choice becomes crucial. If you have tried this technique before and found it a bit tough to deliver, try using different synonyms in the technique to sound more natural in your ears and the customer's.

Let's look at the following examples of how a salesperson might respond to the customer:

Salesperson: James, I can understand why you are telling me this. We've heard this from other office managers before. And what they found was . . . .

Salesperson: . . . by simply trying our service on two occasions, customers found the carpet was not only cleaner, it was fresher smelling, too. What are your thoughts about that?

Another mistake salespeople make when they try to use this technique is that they talk too much during the benefit section of responding to the objection. For example:

Salesperson: James, I can understand . . . other customers found that not only did they enjoy cleaner carpets with our service, they had a pleasant-spring fragrance in the office that increased productivity and remarkably . . . .

This type of response is too long, especially over the phone, and the salesperson just risked the customer checking out. Since they can't see you, customers have to focus harder to understand you. Long spiels are too difficult for them to follow. They sound like a sales pitch, and not a very convincing one, at that!

Confirmation

Salespeople sometimes err in thinking that if a response has covered an objection for them, it is covered for the customer. Not necessarily so. You need to ask the question for confirmation to know that. The customer will not volunteer that he or she is satisfied and ready to buy. You must conduct your check-in every time you answer an objection, regardless of the technique you use in handling the objection.

Here are some examples:

- ▲ "How do you feel about that?"

- ▲ "Will that fly with the boss?"

- ▲ "What do you think about this idea?"

- ▲ "Will that work for you?"

- ▲ "How does that sound?"

Once you secure a solid confirmation, you can move right into the close.

Salesperson: If we can clean carpets using environmentally safe products, and do away with the odor that bothers you, will you give us a try?

Now that's a close that works.

Situational Stress Management

Okay, for those of you who still feel like you may get a bit stressed when customers object, the following tips can help you to stay calm and in control.

Tip 1 *Anticipate, anticipate, anticipate.* Just as remembering to bring insect repellent on the camping trip can prevent the discomfort of battling mosquitoes, preparing for objections can lessen stress considerably.

Tip 2 *Practice with colleagues, a tape recorder, and customers.* Yes, even with customers! Learn what works. It is a mistake, though, to just write down or silently read over and over a list of potential objections and their counters. Even though the non–face-to-face nature of the phone interaction would allow you to do this, customers will pick up on the canned sound of what you are saying.

You will be much more relaxed and effective if you practice saying your responses aloud. This sets up the recall system in your brain, so you don't suffer from test anxiety. Objections feel like a test to us, just like when we were in school. And we can't afford to have our mind go blank when we face objections. If you anticipate questions, know the answers and practice recalling *and saying* them so that you can handle objections skillfully.

Tip 3 *Pause.* Avoid rushing into a response to any objection. Give yourself a few seconds to think about the exchange. Take a moment to get into the customer's perspective. Think about what may be on the customer's mind. If the customer buys a product that is too slow in delivery, proves to be faulty, or is overpriced, then that customer, who is accountable to others, may fear making a buying mistake, especially purchasing from a salesperson over the phone. Fear drives many customers' objections; if something isn't right, customer Linda or Larry may be left holding the bag long after you have collected your commission. (See the discussion of buyer anxiety and risk in Chapter 10)

Tip 4 *No matter how ridiculous you might think the objection is, or even if you think it is a smokescreen (a false objection to get rid of you), take it seriously.* For the customer it may truly be a concern. So, your professional and affirming manner of handling it may not only dispel that particular concern but may earn you serious credibility points and more closed sales down the road.

Tip 5 *Clear the smoke.* Speaking of smokescreens, they come in many forms. Your customer might feel obligated to object, even if there is no real concern. After all, a customer doesn't want you to feel like he or she is easy prey. Price is such a classic brush-off (every customer uses this one, so it should be our first learned objection counter) that it is easy for a customer to just throw it out there. Remember, if you haven't established value for each individual customer, price is irrelevant. Also, if a customer doesn't want to do something, one reason is as good as another.

Tip 6   *Use personality-matching strategies.* As soon as you determine the personality type you are dealing with (**P, E, A,** or **K**), many techniques for managing that person's objections can come to your aid. Plan and prepare for handling customer objections before making the closing phone call. Having a strategy in place will make the difference between a brush-off and a closed sale.

If you tried a technique that worked, try it again. However, make sure you are considering the customer's personality style.

Personality-Type Objection Patterns

In the paragraphs that follow are guidelines on what kinds of objections to expect from each personality type. Also, you will find handling those objections easier than you might have thought.

Precise

Precise people, because they are cautious, have the most objections, both in number and obscurity. Be prepared for this. They will sound skeptical, detailed, and even nitpicky to your ears. The **P** will sound doubtful and will be difficult to read over the phone because the voice quality is flatter, more monotone. The more technical **P** customer will go for the details. If your equipment has a 0.1 percent failure rate, the **Precise** will say, "What if we get the product that is defective?"

The **P** might spend ten minutes questioning you about the failure rate. These customers might "what if" you to death. (Patience is a virtue!) Maybe it's your perception that they are just putting up a smokescreen, but their real concern is that every contingency is being covered. Each objection must be handled precisely, accurately, and honestly.

To Handle Keep your emotions in check. Use facts to respond to objections. Do not talk down to this customer, even if you think he or she might not understand the technical details. Use proof in the form of white papers, third-party testimonials from objective sources (such as *Consumer's Reports*) expert testimony, spec sheets, failure/success rates, anything you can use to demonstrate the proof. Since businesses have separate connections for computers and phones, you can instantly e-mail an article or send the customer to a Web site while you are still on the phone and discuss the proof document at that moment. After all, these are the most critical customers and they don't generally buy into a salesperson's suggestions immediately.

While handling the objection and dealing with the proof, e-mailed or faxed as you speak, lead the customer to the facts in a brochure, on a virtual spec sheet, or on a walk-through of your or other Web sites for details. Last, provide time for this customer to think and make an informed decision. He or she is your most skeptical buyer.

Energized

Energized customers are sloppy with their objections. The poorest of listeners, their objections will sound emotional, yet assertive and quick, maybe even too hasty and not clearly thought out. Also they will attempt to retain the relationship even during the objections with phrases like, "Please, don't take this personally." They might say, "I'm sure you're the top of your field, but we can only afford the middle. You're going to have to give me a break."

Or they may try and persuade you to make special circumstances. "You know we've been doing business with your company for a long time. Doesn't that afford us an extra deal once in a while?"

To Handle Keep your own enthusiasm up. Emphasize value. Demonstrate how your service will make the decision maker look good, personally. Use humor with the **E**'s objection, but not in a sarcastic, offensive way. Humor here is better used for rapport building—something you could both laugh at to assist in building a bond.

Assured

Assureds will get right to the point with objections, sometimes phrased almost as a challenge. They may just object for the fun of it because they like to win and will negotiate as sport. The actual wording of the objection might sound mean over the phone, but remember, it is a game to them. Because **A**s are abrupt, you will hear the objections briefly and assertively pronounced. For example, they might say, "Fred, your price is just way out of line." The **A**s don't sugarcoat their message: "Can't afford you" or "Nope, won't work."

You need to recognize what is really happening; the **A**s *have* to negotiate. They sound unmoving and are generally motivated by feeling like they've won. (And if an **A** doesn't feel like he or she has won, you've lost the deal. Period.)

If you are an **A** yourself, this would be stimulating, because you enjoy a challenge, too. If you are a **Kind**, though, it might be very stressful to deal with this type. Resist the urge to take the **A**'s objection personally. It's not about *you*.

To Handle Sound very confident; do not flounder, waffle, or hesitate. Answer factually; don't get emotional. Tie your response to the needs and objectives you know that they have, then add value for the **A**. Remember, never let an **A** hear you sweat. Since you are on the phone, you can use the advantage of that shield from the **A**'s piercing look to respond with quiet assertion.

If you are selling carpet cleaning, and the **A** customer says,

> **"Why should I pay $500 per office when I can get it done for $300?"**

Respond with,

> **"Because we use chemicals that are nontoxic, eliminating the stench that you find offensive. Not only that, we are faster than the competition due to state-of-the-art cleaning equipment, so you'll have less down time. You'll see the**

difference immediately." Pause. Then ask, "What do you think of that?"

Sometimes you can even challenge them back right on the phone. "The last time you had your offices cleaned by the lowest bidder, what kind of results did you get?" As long as you are still involved in the conversation, you have a chance of closing the business. Keep the conversation going with questions and added value to the transaction.

Kind

Kinds don't want to hurt feelings, and sometimes this makes them harder to deal with, especially in phone conversations, since these people prefer face-to-face interactions. **Kinds** dislike telling you no. Hidden objections often are not related to their voiced objection. If you could see a **Kind** objecting, you would notice the physical cues of squirming and avoiding eye contact, but you will have to listen for verbal phrasing to clue you in on the phone.

Objections a **K** might use include the following:

▲ "I don't know if I can get this past my boss."

▲ "It sounds good, but we just had our carpets cleaned not too long ago."

▲ "Will you send me a brochure?"

▲ "We'll just have to review the options as a team."

The hidden objection might be any number of things: The price is off, they don't like your manner, or the prospect is not the decision maker. Putting you off is easier for a **K** than directing you to the real point of resistance. It's possible that there is no intention or desire to change, but the **K** still wants to be nice to you. You may even hear distress in the **K**'s voice on the phone. Also, keep in mind that the **K** is a slow, cautious decision maker. It takes longer to close this customer, so you may just need to work on him or her over a longer period of time to secure the business.

At some point, you need to uncover the true objection without challenging this person. If you get a lot of "maybe" or "yes" answers, but the prospect will not close or ask for follow-up calls, this is probably a **Kind** who has decided no, but doesn't want to hurt your feelings. You have to then decide whether it's worth pursuing. Look at the relationship, needs, authority, and time-sensitivity of your situation.

To Handle Empathize and make it as personal as possible by using your gentle and confident tone. Also, get the **K**'s coworkers involved. **K**s like to bring in their team, so the responsibility of the decision isn't left entirely up to them.

Salesperson: Mary, I can see where this decision might put you in a tight situation, since you've had a relationship with your current supplier. Let's see how we can make this easier for you and your office staff to make a transition.

Then you will have to review your questioning notes or begin again to uncover the true objection.

The Payoff

Whether you are responding with the questioning technique, incorporating personality types into your strategy, or just preparing to make a call to a new customer, your perception of objections can affect the entire sales call. Remember that objections are just hurdles, not walls. When you get to one, don't stop; size it up and jump— right through the phone lines with your strategy. Expect objections every time, so handling them is not a big deal. Get used to them. This is part of sharpening your sales performance skills.

The more effective you become at handling objections, the more effective you'll be in your selling career, regardless of what you sell. Remember, handling objections effectively is a *learned* skill. "I'm just not good at this part . . ." isn't a valid observation. No one is born an expert at handling objections, so the more you study and practice, the better you will be. Ready? Set? Go!

Negotiating the Close

BLARING TRUMPETS, screaming guitars, or frenzied violins can signal the crescendo or high point of a musical performance. They can also be the ending, or cadence, that is, a blaze of glory finale, perhaps. Other compositions go past that peak of excitement and follow with a winding down to a musical resolution. This puts the listeners in a relaxed and content state as they leave the performance hall.

Sales, as a profession, often attracts people who love the rush and high of the close, the final culmination of prospecting, planning, and managing the customer-selling process. This is a good thing as long as the customer is left with the same excitement about the purchase decision after he or she is no longer on the phone with you, as long as the customer also feels satisfied with the resolution in the transaction.

You will not have the customer "with you" at the close unless he or she has been "with you" during your entire call. As long as you are talking away and passively waiting for the customer to interrupt you to object or say yes, you are not guiding the sales conversation. If you do not keep the customer involved by asking questions throughout the sales conversation, you may have little idea what has excited the customer in your presentation, especially over the phone. So, the close becomes just a shot in the dark, an unsupported guess, with all the stress and uncertainty that can create.

The close does not have to be that way; instead, it can be the natural result of a partnership between you and the customer that serves your goal (the purchase decision) and meets the customer's needs (a solution).

Avoid Dangling Features

As a professional salesperson, you know all about features and benefits. It's just like everyone knows that you wash your hands after going to the bathroom. So, you would never have a dangling feature—saying a feature without immediately including a benefit—would you? Of course not. So, are you doing the **feature → benefit → check-in** process (referred to as the F-B-C formula)? The check-in is where you find out how the customer truly feels about what you have just said and you learn the significance of your particular feature to the client.

A feature is a fact, such as: "We have 24/7 customer service," or "Our company has won nine product excellence awards," or "We deliver to your doorstep within twenty-four hours." Any feature may represent a benefit to most of our customers. And customers usually aren't listening as closely as we'd like on the other end of the phone. That's why it's critical that we include a very specific benefit (or benefits) to the customer after each feature is presented. That's why we must always include the benefit statement (what's in it for them) after each feature.

The Five Benefits

Here is a shortcut for you; there are basically only five benefits in the business world, regardless of what you sell:

1. Saving time
2. Saving money
3. Increasing revenue
4. Reducing stress
5. Improving productivity

There might be specifics related to an industry, such as reducing head count or handling waste, but they can all translate into one of these five benefits. Resist the urge to talk too much when presenting a benefit to a customer. It's easy for a customer to get lost in the verbiage and tune out, even when what you're saying is correct.

Last, *every time* you mention the benefit to your customer, include a phrase such as: "And what this means to you is . . ." or "And the benefit to you is . . ." or "What you'll get out of this is. . . ."

In the case of resellers, though, we have to use a two-layer approach for stating benefits. For example, if an original equipment manufacturer (OEM) makes cell phones for a cellular service company, the OEM has two levels of need he must satisfy. Level one is the direct operational or market advantage benefit. If you are selling a scratchproof plastic for the cover of the cell phone that is inexpensive and easy to fabricate, the benefit to the OEM is lower operational costs on the manufacture of the phone.

However, the level-two benefit is the market advantage he can offer to resellers with the scratchproof case, something the reseller's customers will appreciate. The true sales pro will recognize and capitalize on the opportunity of meeting two levels of need, thus cementing the benefit advantage in the eyes of the customer and making it easier for him to buy.

To us, some benefits of our products may seem to be dramatic differentiators from our competition. However, we must find out how they help the customer we are on the phone with at that moment. Start moving away from plain vanilla, generic benefits and remember to check in with your customers.

Check In

In face-to-face sales calls, we have the ability to read the nonverbal cues, to see what benefits have hit home. Over the phone, it is impossible to know what the customer is really thinking, unless you use a method of regularly checking in for customer reaction. Since not all reactions are audible comments, you are challenged with monitoring where the customer is by asking questions *during* the presentation portion of your call; you are "checking in" to determine the customer's acceptance level. Another advantage of this check-in technique is that as you are keeping your customer involved, he or she is far less likely to be drifting away from your conversation by multitasking during the call.

If door-to-door delivery (feature) is supposed to improve productivity (benefit), the customer could be thinking, "I don't care about delivery right to my door. I want delivery to our remote warehouse." So, not every benefit plays as an advantage to the customer unless you have *specifically tied the benefit to the customer's business.* Customers won't tell us if we've missed, rather they will just tune out.

The check-in allows us to find out where we stand.

Think of it this way. If you go to dentist for a filling, he gives you a shot. Then, he asks you if it still hurts; if it does, he'll give you another shot. If you don't tell the dentist that the pain is still there, he won't give you another shot to reduce pain. The check-in technique lets you find out how your customer feels about the benefit you have just offered.

Let's go back to the feature of door-to-door delivery with the benefits, for example, of saving time and improving productivity. Your check-in might include asking one of the following questions:

▲ "Harry, how do you feel about that?"

▲ "Lenore, when can you use this to your advantage?"

▲ "William, on a scale of one to ten, how important is that to you?"

If the customer's response is positive on that benefit, you have now added value and can often close the sale on the customer's response. The result of your check-in tells you what to focus on in your presentation. When you frame your presentation in this way, you set yourself up for success by eliminating objections. Throughout your entire presentation, you are gaining interaction and buy-in. This is far superior to the *feature-dump* or *benefit-dump* approach, especially over the phone when you don't know if your customer is even listening.

If the customer's answer is negative, obviously the feature and benefit aren't important to this particular customer. Then, you'll go to the next important feature and define it as a benefit related to your customer's needs. Work harder at uncovering matches, not at dogging the issue to try to convince the customer that the feature you just suggested is important. Even if it is important to *all* other customers in your experience, *move on.* Even if you think the customer is an idiot for not seeing the obvious value of the feature, *move on.* You can make the situation adversarial by hanging on, resulting in a lost sale.

> **It doesn't matter if all your other customers value a specific feature, the *only* concern that you should have is *this customer* in *this call.***

Remember **F-B-C,** or feature → benefit → check-in. If you get all positives, you can go to a close at any time, often without any objections. Also, don't rely on the benefits list the marketing team or your sales manager has given you. A benefit is what it means to *your* customer, not to a generic customer.

I-N-V-O-L-V-E Your Customer

Today's customers have about a thirteen-second attention span. What to do? Keep the customer involved. It is especially important in phone selling to get the customer involved right from the start.

Here are the steps you need to take for maintaining that the customer is indeed listening, paying attention, *and* thinking of buying from you. The acronym INVOLVE will help you remember what to do.

I = Interest your customer. Do you have a colorful story, a satisfied customer you can bring in for a conference call testimonial, product comparison that you can fax during the conversation, or a Web site you can refer the customer to while you are talking? These enhancements to the call get your customer's attention. Try something that your competition has never tried before. Do something different to help create excitement and to establish your creativity as a professional during your presentation. Have some fun with it; your customer will, too!

N = Never use the phrase, "I think," during your presentation. Why? Your customers don't care what *you* think. They only care about what *they* think. Customers sometimes relate to your other customers, and may want to know about others' experiences or challenges. However, never tell your customers what you think, because in their minds—right or not—*you* are on commission and your ideas are less than credible.

V = Verbally keep the customer involved by asking questions during your phone presentation, such as: "What do you think of that idea?" and "How much do you think that will save you in the long run?" or "Where can you use this?"

O = Organize your thoughts before presenting over the phone. Remember today's customers and their very short attention spans? You'd better be prepared to be succinct, focus on this particular customer's specific needs, and not talk too much. The better organized you are, the less chance you'll talk yourself right out of a sale! Customers remember in threes, so organize to focus on three specific selling points. You can open with, "Ms. Solumba, there are three main features you might find interesting in your situation."

L = Let you customer interrupt. If your customer is (a) excited or (b) bored, you may be interrupted. If the customer is excited, great! Close the sale right there. If the customer is bored, she's telling you to move on to another point—that the one you're spending too much time on has lost her interest and isn't important to her. Remember that you can't see boredom or excitement over the phone, so you need to listen carefully to the customer's tone and pause frequently to pull the customer's comments into the conversation.

V = Verify that what you are presenting are, indeed, the right ideas to suit your customer's most pressing needs. How do you do this? By listening. Did the customer agree, interrupt, or cut you off? Listen for the clues and follow through with some ideas of your own. Remember to write down what the customer is saying in his or her own words throughout your call.

E = Express yourself skillfully. If you are emphasizing how your service worked with another customer, tell a story to make it interesting and compelling to the customer. If you focus on your customer's real need, you avoid rambling and establish your credibility. You'll find that the sale is just around the corner.

Use Storytelling

Customers respond to stories that give them past history or emphasize success. They remember stories that emphasize your product and how well that product has worked. If you sell heating and air-conditioning systems, and your systems are less expensive to maintain in the long term than your competition's, tell a story about a customer who saved 20 percent in maintenance costs over a five-year period. Be quick, short, and to the point.

Rules for stories that provide your customer with proof include:

▲ Must be true because your customer may ask for more information or a reference

▲ Must be short, two to three sentences

▲ Should establish your credibility and compliment the customer

▲ Should not directly address your competitor's weaknesses or flaws

▲ Must be practiced to ensure smooth and effective delivery

The implication is, "Customer, you are smart like our other smart customers, so you will want to use our product in just the same way."

We refer to this as providing a third-party testimonial, which is more effective than offering *your* opinion over the phone. You are now simply (yet importantly) the messenger for a positive experience another customer has enjoyed by conducting business with you. Customers are much better informed today than they used to be. Buyers are more sophisticated these days because of easy availability of information (just look at how much you can learn about products on the Web). You're not going to put anything past the customer, so go instead for a story you know or an experience with which you are familiar.

Drop Names

It is important to know when to name-drop to help you close more sales. If you are talking to a smaller company, compare other customers that are approximately the same size, provided they're not direct competitors. When you are talking with a Fortune 100 company, name-drop other 100s or 500s that are similar—they may be in the same industry but just not direct competitors. For example, a frozen-food distributor and a canned-food distributor are the same industry, and may even have some of the same customers; however, they are not competing directly.

If there is someone your customer knows and likes, this is an excellent name to drop. For example, if you are selling helpdesk services to a company, you might use the internal contact's name with whom you are already doing business. You need to know in advance that the two people like each other. If you don't have this information, however, you run the risk of using a negative association and possibly losing the sale.

Never use name-dropping if what you sell is too confidential or if the situation requires extreme discretion. If your customer's name is a direct competitor, don't use it. If the company may be offensive or insulting in your customer's eyes, don't use it. If the products are too different or unrelated (like pet foods and airplane parts), don't use the company name. However, if you are selling solutions, tie the significant and relevant elements of the story into your presentation.

Eliminate Buyer Anxiety

Whatever customers buy from you—whether it is computer equipment or maintenance products—individuals feel accountable for the purchase. If a buyer purchases computer systems that fail to perform up to standards or cleaning supplies that have an offensive odor, buyers fear some sort of reprisal for a bad decision: loss of respect, ridicule, or even a reprimand. That is part of customers' price consideration—it's not just the dollar expense, it's the *professional* expense.

The professional salesperson understands the total cost that the customer is considering. This is **price + risk.** Using a process format to guide the sales cycle ensures that the sale will stick. In other words, by eliminating your buyer's anxiety, you ensure that there won't be excessive returns or afterthought cancellations, all of which cost you money in short-term business and, more important, in long-term dollars.

Overcoming the voiced objections is straightforward, but this perceived risk element is something you may have to surmise or uncover on your own. You won't be able to see a concerned expression on your prospect's face, so taking into account the personality-style aspects of perceived risk and buyer anxiety and listening closely to the customer's tone and/or silence will help you.

Anticipate Personality and Risk

Considering how important your customers *real* thoughts are, you'll want to pay close attention to differing personality stress points.

Precise

Since the **P** is generally overly cautious, fact-oriented, and avoids change, any lack of preparedness on your part or absence of data will cause this customer's risk meter to jump. **P**s are *extremely* risk averse, but often respected for their concern with informational detail. Although often not the final decision maker, the **P**'s input will be regarded with seriousness and can quickly kill a deal if negative. **P**s especially enjoy being perceived as the expert. Thus, making a mistake and losing the esteem of colleagues would be too high a price for a **P** to pay. The phone is the perfect medium for handling a **P** because they are more interested in data than in knowing you anyway.

Risk-Management Strategy Make certain that the **P** has a load of data, such as product samples, white papers, demos, third-party testimonials, financial date, articles from trade journals, test results, and anything else you can provide when you make your call. If the **P** is convinced of your product's merit, however, he or she will sell for you in decision-maker meetings. They go about this by digging in their heels and swearing up and down that the decision they've researched, is indeed, the *correct* one. In group decision making meetings, the **P**s are not necessarily the most popular, but their opinions are well respected.

Energized

Energized customers are emotional and can buy in the heat of the moment on impulse. So, at first glance, the **Energized** customer may seem to be a risk taker. This can work for or against you; buyer's remorse is no stranger to the **E** customer because of this excited impulsivity.

Thus, the professional risk for the **E** is the potential to be thought foolish by the boss or coworkers. With jobs as precarious as they are these days, the **E** customer may even fear losing a job if the decision is disastrously wrong. For this reason, **E**s may bring a coworker or co-decision-maker into the situation—generally someone with a different personality style. Buying because it "felt right" may have gotten your **E** customer into real trouble at some point in the past.

Risk-Management Strategy Get excited along with the **E**s; let them hear it in your voice, and show these customers that their decision will make them look good. Deepen the relationship with regular follow-up contacts, so that you become a trusted partner. When a third party is brought in, you can likely assume that the **E** has already decided in your favor. So, when you talk to this third party, it might be a good idea to have the **E**, whom you've already convinced, on the speaker phone or conference call. Your job will be to handle the other person and to reassure the **E** that the decision is good one and that he or she will personally benefit.

Also, remember **E** customers lose things, so always have an extra copy of the agreement in a brightly colored organizational folder to send as a follow-up to your call, and e-mail messages with backup data in case you need to resend information and to assist this **E** customer in keeping track of your "stuff." *Note:* this also gives you a legitimate excuse to make a call back to the **E** to ensure that he or she has received what you have sent. Use this callback to reiterate the solidness of the product and to appeal to the **E**'s real motivator—*recognition.*

Assured

Since **A**s see themselves as innovators and live by taking risks, these customers may appear to have no buyer anxiety. Truly, they generally only fear being bested in a deal: a major blow to an **A**. An **A** who finds no room to negotiate will see this as too confining and may walk away from a deal.

Assureds, though, are often politically motivated in their organizations. They may put you on speakerphone if someone important is in their office when you call. If their anxiety level is high, they may become arrogant on the phone and you can hear that in your **A**'s voice. Just remember, the price of the sale for the **Assured** customer will include career impact as well. **A**s may love conflict and negotiating with you, but probably would chafe at the possibility of a bad purchase costing them politically. So make them look good.

Risk-Management Strategy Remind the **A** often that he or she is getting a great deal. Be prepared to negotiate and not necessarily have the upper hand. You may want to hold something back at the beginning of a negotiation in order to spring it as a freebie later. When the **Assured** makes a decision, it may be marked only with a terse "okay." Don't talk too much over the close, or you might cause the **Assured** to rethink the wisdom of the decision. He or she is ready to move on; you should be, too.

Kind

Kind customers fear confrontation, negotiation, and risk. They would walk miles out of their way to avoid these if necessary. Discord and the prospect of someone's feelings or situation being hurt by their actions are almost painful. They will buy a Saturn car just for its no-haggle policy. As young people, **Kinds** were very naïve and trusting, but if they have been taken advantage of enough times, they will see every deal as risky. Sadly, they begin to doubt their judgment, and they fear making a mistake.

Because of this, the **Kind**, like the **Energized**, will probably bring in a partner or a committee as protective armor for the decision—generally a **P**, who will slow the process or an **A**, who acts as a hard-nosed negotiator.

Risk-Management Strategy Slow down! You will have to earn the trust of the **K** unless you want all dealings with him or her to be group decisions. Remember to use your voice in a more supportive and soothing way, rather than in a crisp and direct style. Walk the **K** through the closing process. For example, a salesperson might say, "Larry, it sounds like our software is right for your application, based on what you told me you liked (1)_____ (2)_____ (3)_____. I can show you how easily it can be implemented in your department." Paint the picture of satisfaction and ease of transition after the sale. List all the steps: "First our systems designer will go over the compatibility issues, then we'll plan the installation (we can do that during your regular shutdown), finally the training—at our expense. We'll have your team up and running in a short time frame."

Show the **Kind** that the decision is a *safe* one. Cover and show plans for alleviating any potential snags. Support them in their decision.

Advance the Sale

When you do everything right during the process, you are always advancing the sale over the phone. Uncover real needs and connect benefits to the customer's unique situation throughout the qualifying process and your customers will make their own decisions based on the ammunition and support you have given them. When you work in tandem with customers, they feel in command of the situation; they *own* the decision. For this reason, the competition will not be able to unseat the sale. Both you and the customer win this way. And long-term repeat business with this customer will be infinitely easier.

Ask for the Business

Closing the business *requires* asking for the order. Customers by nature will not say, "I am selecting you for this project." They will, however, give you clues to the correct timing. Remember, if you have qualified correctly and established a good consultative relationship, you can close at any time during the process. All you need is enough yes responses on your check-ins. Listen for the tone of the yes responses as well; make sure it's a yes of assent, not just to get you off the phone.

When a customer says any of the following comments, go for your close:

- ▲ "That sounds good."
- ▲ "I like the ideas that you are sharing."
- ▲ "Maybe it *is* time for a change."
- ▲ "This is the best solution I've seen so far."

You'll still need to *ask* for the business, though, in order to get it! So, you need to respond with one of the following statements:

- ▲ "It sounds like we have the solution for you. Are you ready to place the order?"
- ▲ "Based on what you've told me, we have a great match. Let's get started on the agreement."
- ▲ "Sounds like you are ready to go. When do you want to take delivery?"
- ▲ "I like what you're telling me. What do you need from me to get going on the implementation?"

The customer may be ready to buy, but you can still expect the possibility of negotiating a few of the final details on the phone call.

Negotiate by Personality

Each personality type approaches the negotiation stage in a different way. Look at the following descriptions.

Assured

They are motivated by the desire to reach *one goal* in the outcome. The **Assured** customer must reach that goal or feel like he or she has lost. Avoid the win/win approach, because if you "win" at all, this customer has "lost."

Quick Notes—Negotiating with the Assured

- ▲ Goal = Victory
- ▲ Negotiation approach = Threatens, demands
- ▲ Style = Hard, maybe even ultimatums
- ▲ Weakness = Digs in and thus may sidestep concessions
- ▲ Requires from you = Position or posture that you are equal

Energized

They are motivated by impulse and the desire to move on. If **Energized** customers feel they have influenced you to change your mind or concede, they have succeeded in the negotiation.

Quick Notes—Negotiating with the Energized

- ▲ Goal = Influence you
- ▲ Negotiation approach = High intensity, may be loud and sound emphatic and energetic
- ▲ Style = Excitable, wants others to be at the same excitement level
- ▲ Weakness = Ignores others, may not listen
- ▲ Requires from you = Ability to maintain enthusiasm, celebration of decision

Kind

They are motivated by the desire to ensure that everyone is happy with the outcome. The **Kind** customer takes a long time to make a decision, and is cautious about the effects on everyone involved.

Quick Notes—Negotiating with the Kind

▲ Goal = Agreement and positive effect all arround
▲ Negotiation approach = Develops relationship
▲ Style = Soft, will accept losses if justified
▲ Weakness = Easily swayed; but cannot be "bullied"
▲ Requires from you = Agreement and reminder that decision is good

Precise

They are motivated by details, details, and more details! **Precise** customers like to have a recognizable structure in the negotiation, with everything buttoned up. They will be put off by any last-minute surprises. Remember also that the **Precise** will want everything in writing!

Quick Notes—Negotiating with the Precise

▲ Goal = Order, structure
▲ Negotiation style = Ignores relationships, rigid
▲ Style = Detached, nitpicky on details
▲ Weakness = Inflexible, predictable
▲ Requires from you = Systematic, organized approach, proofs—support

Seal the Close

Sales have been lost on more than one occasion because of inattention from the salesperson after the customer's initial verbal purchase agreement. Every salesperson has experienced the customer who has backed out of a deal, especially when it's an agreement over the phone. A simple "yes" may set you up for celebration, but you are not done until you take that one final step of sealing the close. Here are some techniques to make those acceptance responses stick.

Verbal

With this type of sealer you celebrate with the customer, by saying effusively:

- ▲ "Great!"
- ▲ "That's terrific news!"
- ▲ "We'll ship this afternoon."
- ▲ "Thank you so much!"
- ▲ "I know management will be pleased"
- ▲ "Wonderful! We can't wait to get started on the project!"

Voice and tone are critical with this close sealer. For some reason, many salespeople get excited internally when they close a sale, but don't want to reveal this to the customer. Show your pleasure verbally right over the phone.

Another holdback on the part of salespeople is not saying thank you. If the customer does not hear your enthusiasm, then he or she may begin to question the decision almost immediately, otherwise known as "buyer's remorse." Sealing the close verbally will keep your competition from overturning the decision after you hang up the phone. Remember to let your customers know that you are acting on their decision and starting the delivery process. Keeping up the momentum after the decision is crucial to sealing the close.

Mailed, Personalized Confirmation

By fax or paper, send a handwritten thank-you note with the contract attached. Or send a note on a card, personalized for your business.

For example, it might say, "I'm delighted to have your business, and I look forward to working with you." Some sort of small gift can be included: a specialty product from your company, a mug, T-shirt, nice pen, or something personalized. Other gifts that might be appropriate include cookies, chocolates with the company name on them, office products, or small samples. Whether you send a gift or not, be sure to send the handwritten note to personalize the thank-you.

Initial Delivery

Get some part of the purchase sent to the customer right away to ensure that the close has progressed. Examples include:

▲ The display rack that goes with the product

▲ Operation manuals

▲ Promotional literature, brochures, and samples for resellers

▲ Several products (if you can't send the five hundred they have purchased, send three)

▲ Cases for the equipment installation

Even if it is just the mats that go under the office chairs or the warranty certificates, whatever you send is delivery on the customer's decision and seals the deal so your customer is unlikely to back out.

The Payoff

Anxiety of both buyer and salesperson at close time can be virtually eliminated with a solid presentation that includes effective qualifying. The close is the natural result of a harmonious, transactional conversation. Salespeople who are tuned in to the personality type and the real needs of customers close the business. They create solid matches and sales that stick, long after they have hung up the phone. Long-term sales relationships create profit for your company while they solve problems for your customers. The close is where you get to cash in on your phone-selling strategy.

Appendix A: PEAK Personality Type Assessment

Personality Profile

Examine the four adjectives in each grouping. Rank the adjective that *best* describes you with a 7, the next closest a 5, the next closest a 3, and the least descriptive adjective with a 1. Use each number only once in each set.

1. _____ (**A**) punctual
   _____ (**E**) enthusiastic
   _____ (**K**) family-oriented
   _____ (**P**) orderly

2. _____ (**A**) adventurous
   _____ (**E**) life of the party
   _____ (**K**) moderate
   _____ (**P**) precise

3. _____ (**A**) stubborn
   _____ (**E**) persuasive
   _____ (**K**) gentle
   _____ (**P**) humble

4. _____ (**A**) competitive
   _____ (**E**) playful
   _____ (**K**) obliging
   _____ (**P**) obedient

5. _____ (**A**) determined
   _____ (**E**) convincing
   _____ (**K**) good-natured
   _____ (**P**) cautious

6. _____ (**A**) assertive
   _____ (**E**) optimistic
   _____ (**K**) lenient
   _____ (**P**) accurate

Add each letter value by transferring the numbers to the bottom of this form below each letter and totaling. (For example, 16 **P**s, 24 **A**s, and so forth.) Note your highest numbers to determine your natural style.

P	E	A	K
_____	_____	_____	_____

Appendix B: Powerful Proposals That Sell

Remember that phone sales works with only one of your customer's information processing channels, and that most customers internalize less than one third of what you say to them. By following up with a written proposal, when the situation warrants it, you will help to ensure that you have sealed the close.

To Prepare

1. Have all your needs assessment questions answered by the customer.

2. Have your ideas clearly thought out and understood so that you can present them in the best light.

3. Have the customers' names spelled correctly.

4. Make sure you know who is to receive copies of the proposal.

5. Use the customer's company colors somewhere in the binder, and as often as possible. (For example, if the customer is The Coca-Cola Company, use red binders, etc.).

6. Focus on the customer benefits throughout the proposal. (For example, "What this means to you is . . . .")

7. Give customers options so that they can make decisions based on variations of *your* company's product offerings.

8. Make the proposal as accessible and interesting as possible. Consider the following ideas:

  ▲ Use a 12-point font for ease of reading.

  ▲ Use colored paper in some places, but don't overdo unless it's for a visual arts type proposal.

  ▲ Use graphics, illustrations, and color—again, don't overdo, but a bar or bullets in blue ink can catch the eye of your reader.

  ▲ Include sample materials: software screen capture, a piece of metal casing, etc.

  ▲ Use colored tabs to make it easier to find information.

  ▲ Remember to place headings at the beginning of each important information section. Decision makers are "skimmers."

  ▲ Put the customer's name on the outside of the binder or folder.

9. Include an Executive Summary in your proposal: a brief one-page synopsis for the quick reader who is interested only in the bottom line. *Put this first* after the Table of Contents page.

10. Make sure you include customer benefits throughout the proposal.

Components of the Proposal

Title Page

Table of Contents Page

Executive Summary

Customer Applications— Situation Analysis or Needs Assessment (Don't use the word *problem*, it's negative and may suggest an insult to the customer.)

Your Company's Capabilities and Solutions

Completed Project Samples (This is what the customer will have when done.)

Product Specifics: Use a great amount of detail for technical customers, more "what it can do" for business decision makers who are less technical.

Frequently Asked Questions

Recommendation: This is where you list the specifics of what the customer is buying. If you include a place to sign, the customer can send this part back to you as a purchase agreement.

References

Appendices: Here is where you put articles in industry publications about your company or its products, also more details of tables or test results, etc., than you had room for in your proposal body.

Table of Contents

Include the page numbers and the major tab headings on this page.

Customer Applications

In this section, you'll provide the overview of the situation as described by the client. Think of this as your customer's problem area. If selling office furniture, it may describe an out-of-date reception area, an ergonomically unsuitable research department of ten employees, an executive office that needs updating and upgrading, or more. Include the emotion behind the problems to which the customer needs a solution. (For example: "The president's office is in need of updating so that he can present the company in the best light; indicating a bright future of company prosperity.")

Remember: This is where you remind the customer of the needs *he* or *she* voiced in your qualifying. Use the customer's words from your notes to describe the situation; that way your "insights" into the problem will ring true.

Capabilities and Solutions

This is an important section, but one that salespeople frequently do badly in presenting. The customer is not interested in your entire company's history, and a generic cut-and-paste from the company's public relations summary or stockholder's report will be seriously ho-hum. Use a razor-sharp editing mind to present *exactly* what the customer will need to solve the problem. Spotlight your company's particular expertise in the area where the customer is most concerned. Here also you will be able to direct the customer to the appendix, where you have strategically placed a few positive articles about your company or the product/service the customer will be purchasing.

In addition, be sure to detail what the situation will be like when your product or service is put into use: "The order processing department will increase order turnaround by 50 percent when the optical character readers are used."

Index

About the Authors

Renee Walkup is the president of SalesPEAK, Inc., her passion since 1996, where she helps her clients boost sales and drive profits through innovative selling techniques. Prior to founding SalesPEAK, Renee won numerous awards as a peak performer for seventeen years in sales and sales management within publishing, software, and other fields. Her clients include The Coca-Cola Company, CNN, Charles Schwab & Co., LaFarge USA, Nestle, Medical Doctor Associates, HMA, International Thomson, and dozens of medium-size companies throughout the world.

Thousands of professionals subscribe to her monthly tips newsletters (available at www.salespeak.com or by calling 678-587-9911), where she provides valuable sales ideas.

A graduate of Stephens College in Missouri, Renee lives in Atlanta, Georgia, with her husband Ted and daughter Rachel.

Sandra McKee has spent the last twenty years of her life helping individuals and companies prepare for and achieve their professional goals. As a speaker and trainer she has worked with Fortune 500 corporations, nonprofits, and small businesses throughout the United States. Currently, she is a senior professor at DeVry University in Atlanta. Sandra is the author of three other internationally published books and the mother of two sons.